A Cancer Survivor's
Physical
&
Spiritual
Journey

A Cancer Survivor's
Physical
& Spiritual
Journey

A. Hodges

ARCHWAY
PUBLISHING

Archway Publishing books may be ordered
through booksellers or by contacting:

Archway Publishing
1663 Liberty Drive
Bloomington, IN 47403
www.archwaypublishing.com
1 (888) 242-5904

Scripture taken from the Holy Bible, NEW INTERNATIONAL
VERSION®. Copyright © 1973, 1978, 1984 by Biblica, Inc. All rights
reserved worldwide. Used by permission. NEW INTERNATIONAL
VERSION® and NIV® are registered trademarks of Biblica, Inc.
Use of either trademark for the offering of goods or services
requires the prior written consent of Biblica US, Inc.

ISBN: 978-1-4808-3563-4 (sc)
ISBN: 978-1-4808-3564-1 (e)

Library of Congress Control Number: 2016912928

Print information available on the last page.

Archway Publishing rev. date: 8/22/2016

ACKNOWLEDGMENTS

A special acknowledgment to close friends and family members who have been with me throughout my difficult journey with this complex cancer.

Beginning with my 2004 cancer diagnosis in Springfield, a note of thanks to all the medical providers and institutions that have contributed to my current status of having successfully tackled this complicated disease. I have progressed from mostly bedridden during 2004 to functioning well in 2016.

A special note of thanks to American Airlines for providing such an excellent retiree medical program. Especially, I thank Winship Cancer Institute of Emory University, Georgia Cancer Specialists, CVS/Caremark specialty pharmacy, Chronic Disease Fund, Emory Saint Joseph's Hospital of Atlanta, Northside Hospital, Emory Healthcare, and all the emergency medical services, physicians, surgeons, pharmacists, anesthesiologists, radiologists, physician assistants, nurses, medical assistants, lab technicians, staff, physical therapists, volunteers, and all other health-care and hospital workers.

I also wish to acknowledge all researchers, developers, and manufacturers of the wonderful medical treatments that are so effective in managing cancer and other terminal illnesses.

CONTENTS

Preface...ix

INTRODUCTION   A Brief Autobiographical Account xi

CHAPTER 1   Diagnosis, Surgery, and Treatment..... 1

CHAPTER 2   The Transport to Atlanta:
Antibiotic Therapy and
Hardware Removal Surgery 9

CHAPTER 3   Continued Oncology Care with
Bone Therapy Treatments................ 15

CHAPTER 4   More Radiation Therapy and
Chemotherapy Treatments............. 19

CHAPTER 5   The Spiritual Connection................25

CONCLUSION   A General Review 31

About the Author 33

Endnotes.. 35

PREFACE

This story details my experience with multiple myeloma, a cancer that, at the time of my diagnosis,
came with a life expectancy of up to five years. I was
diagnosed at age fifty-five, and I'm still here almost
twelve years later, at age sixty-seven. My treatment
process has consisted of radiation therapy, chemotherapy, and ongoing bone therapy treatments.
Presently, my quality of life is good.

After a brief introduction, I will describe the
circumstances surrounding my cancer diagnosis.
Looking back several years later, after many notewor-
thy experiences and occurrences related to the cancer,
I realized the spiritual connection. After detailing
the physical (sometimes nearly fatal) phase of my experience in chapters 1 through 4, in chapter 5 I will

discuss this extraordinary spiritual discovery, while I seek to demonstrate an empirical relationship, citing phenomenology, a philosophical school of thought.

My story reflects my personal experiences and opinions, and not those of any of my acknowledgements or references. Although the book is not meant to be instructive, I hope the reader finds my story helpful and informative.

A Brief Autobiographical Account

I was born in Mississippi. In the early fifties, my family moved from the southern part of the United States to the Midwest, settling in Saginaw, Michigan. At that time, work in many Northern industrial cities was plentiful, particularly in the steel and automobile industries.

In 1965, after graduating from high school at age seventeen, I took a summer job in my hometown of Saginaw. A major retailer hired me to work as a part-time salesgirl.

After completing secretarial training courses at a business school in Saginaw, in 1967 I became a full-time employee of Michigan's power company, where I worked in the local executive office, specifically for the two engineers in the bulk power division. One engineer was in charge of the local mechanical engineering division, and the other was in charge of the local electrical engineering division. I was the stenographer for both engineers.

The stenographer was in charge of the general office duties, including taking shorthand dictation and typing letters. Through the hallway was the office of the vice president and his secretary; at the end of the hallway sat the division president with his executive secretary.

Although the environment was pleasant, after working there for two years I was ready to try something different. Acting on the suggestion of a close friend, I began exploring the occupation of airline stewardess. I was accepted for stewardess training by two major airlines, and in 1971 I was hired by the one I had initially preferred: American Airlines. American, in my opinion, had the prettiest airplanes.

The job title was eventually changed from stewardess to flight attendant. Either way, it was a great travel experience and, for me, a way to complete my college education, thanks to both the convenience of the scheduling process and the salary that helped pay for the tuition. The scheduling procedures were conducive to my flying on the weekends and attending college/university classes during the week.

From 1971 to 1973, my crew base was in New York City, where I flew out of three airports: LGA, JFK, and EWR. In July of 1973, I transferred to the Chicago crew base, ORD. Shortly afterward, I began my studies at the Loop College, one of the City Colleges of Chicago (now Harold Washington College), where I completed an associate in arts degree. From there, I went on to complete my bachelor of arts degree at Northeastern Illinois University, Chicago, and my master of arts degree at DePaul University, Chicago.

My airline career spanned two and a half decades, from June 1971 through January 1996. The majority of that time was spent in Illinois, where I resided primarily in Evanston. Eventually, I sold my home in Evanston and relocated from Cook County to Sangamon County, Springfield. I'm currently retired in Georgia.

CHAPTER 1

Diagnosis, Surgery, and Treatment

On January 24, 2004, in one of the upstairs bedrooms at my home in Springfield, I had started to routinely lie down in bed for sleep. Suddenly, I felt no sensation from the waist down. I immediately reached for the phone and dialed 911. Sliding onto the floor on my stomach, I used my arms to pull myself to the stairway and on downstairs while dragging my lower body.

During this critical time, I did not panic. I simply focused on the steps I needed to take in order to get to a hospital for medical care. I felt neither pain nor any tingling sensation, only numbness in my lower extremities.

By the time I reached the bottom of the stairs, the emergency medical services team was at the door. I reached up to unlock the door, and they entered. Not only did they respond very quickly, but carefully secured my home prior to leaving.

There were two major hospitals in Springfield: Memorial Medical and St. John's Hospital. When asked by the ambulance driver which hospital I preferred to go to, I instinctively said, "St. John's." I can think of no specific reason why.

On arriving at the hospital's emergency room, I was wheeled to an examining room and afterward to an operating room, where I slowly lost consciousness after being administered anesthesia. After scribbling my signature onto the consent forms, I awoke in the intensive care unit after undergoing thoracic and lumbar surgeries, and a tumor was removed; a posterior cervical laminectomy with fusion and stabilization was performed. Afterward, the orthopedic surgeon from Springfield Clinic placed a rod in the top area of my back. After the surgical procedures, my height went from five feet four and one-half inches to five feet two inches.

After awakening, I was mentally alert while consulting with the oncologist. He informed me of my cancer diagnosis: stage IIA multiple myeloma. Terminal, he said. Treatable, but not curable.

Prior to that date, I had never heard of multiple myeloma. It is a cancer of the blood that begins in the plasma cells in bone marrow (the soft, spongy tissue located in the center of many bones where blood cells are produced).[1] Malignant plasma cells can lead to tumors, kidney disease, and interference with the body's ability to fight infections.

Retired after long-term employment in the private sector (corporate), along with pursuing my academic endeavors, my life on earth has been a life of fulfillment. Reflecting on my experiences from young adulthood through middle age, if my passing on had happened at the time of my cancer diagnosis, I would have gone without regrets. Therefore, I took the news about my disability calmly and fearlessly. With no fear of death, I felt neither sadness nor anxiety, merely a need to put things in order.

Being a physically active and very independent person, I always thought that any suggestion of the inability to use my limbs would be frightening and devastating. For many years, I had not only been self-supporting but routinely walked for exercise and frequently rode my bicycle. Yet even with this, to my surprise, I remained calm and fearless.

Since I perceive death to be a transition into another phase of life rather than the absence of life—that is, a transformation from the material world of flesh, blood, and bones to a purely spiritual, nonmaterial existence—I contend that my perception of death contributed to my having no fear or regrets about passing. Ultimately, what prepared me for readiness when the time came was my knowledge of the existence of that perpetual state of goodness and love called Heaven.

Since my diagnosis, I have spent more time with family—specifically my brother and sister who both left Michigan in the seventies to pursue their careers in Georgia. My career, as stated in my Introduction, led to my settling in Illinois in the early seventies. Of course, over the years, my siblings and I had stayed in touch as much as possible; however, as a consequence of my illness, we spent more quantity as well as quality time together.

I awoke in the hospital in January to discover that not only did I have terminal cancer, with its unrecognizable symptoms, but I was also paralyzed from the waist down. It was uncertain as to whether I would ever walk again. The lack of sensation that I experienced in the lower part of my body was due to the paralysis. In turn, a tumor was found in my lumbar region.

My family was notified. My two sisters immediately came to Springfield. The hospital provided lots of support through local churches. Volunteers assisted with household chores and errands. My American Airlines retiree medical insurance, along with AA supplemental medical, adequately covered me for the first two years of my illness. In February 2006, two years after my cancer diagnosis, coverage switched automatically from retiree medical to Medicare, which became my primary insurance.

I must stress the importance of having health insurance regardless of one's current health condition. As noted, prior to my cancer diagnosis, I was healthy and active.

As I moved in and out of the hospital and home health care, I pondered my existence and accepted the idea of being permanently wheelchair bound. Then a little thought, an inner voice, came to my mind that said, *Put one foot in front of the other.*

After the surgeries, I was sent to Memorial Medical

for intense physical therapy, which proved to be very effective. In just a few weeks, I began experiencing movement in my lower extremities. Beginning with a wiggle of the big toe on my right foot, movement gradually returned to all of my lower body. I graduated from the wheelchair to a walker and then to a cane. Presently, very cautiously, I can walk without a cane.

While still using a wheelchair, I received radiation therapy at St. John's Hospital. Soon after, an extremely large hole developed in the back of my neck, which was determined to be a cervical wound described in hospital notes as "an open wound in the dorsal aspect of the neck."

I was readmitted into St. John's Hospital several times for wound dehiscence. A vacuum-assisted closure was placed. The attending physician/surgeon was from the Southern Illinois University (SIU) medical group, and a visiting nurse was sent to my home to treat the wound with wet-to-dry dressings.

I was frequently hospitalized in 2004. In April, a staph infection was found in the wound (the culture is described in hospital notes as "many staphylococcus aureus"). The list of recommended antibiotic treatments included clindamycin, gentamycin, penicillin G, and vancomycin. Home health care continued with the wet-to-dry dressings. During this time, as I attempted to turn my car's steering wheel, the steering column felt as though it was locked. My car had power steering, and I had never experienced problems turning the wheel. I simply assumed that I would probably not be able to drive again based on my medical condition.

Also in 2004, I received chemotherapy treatments. At the time, the treatments for multiple myeloma were Velcade and Doxil. Both chemotherapy drugs were administered intravenously. According to the SIU oncologist, the next step would be a stem cell transplant, performed by him. However, my retiree medical insurance program had two hospitals in the area that were approved for stem cell transplantation therapy: one in Chicago and the other in St. Louis. Since my closest family members were in Atlanta, I inquired about and was referred to a facility in the Atlanta area that was approved by my medical plan for the stem cell transplant.

CHAPTER 2

The Transport to Atlanta: Antibiotic Therapy and Hardware Removal Surgery

The approved facility was at Northside Hospital—the Blood and Marrow Transplant Group of Georgia. In the winter of 2005, I began preparations for travel to Atlanta for the stem cell transplantation therapy.

My condition was poor, and I moved very slowly. With the large hole in the back of my neck, I could barely hold up my head. I wondered how, in that condition, I could possibly board an airplane to travel

A. HODGES

from Illinois to Georgia. Because of my degraded condition, travel by ground was out of the question—it would take far too long.

Thanks to the ease and convenience of the BMI regional airport and its carriers with nonstop flights between Bloomington and Atlanta—and, of course, to my sister who escorted me throughout the entire trip—I eventually arrived safely at Hartsfield-Jackson Atlanta International Airport. We were met by a friend who drove us to my sister's house. Once inside, I stopped in the living room and laid on my back on the couch, wondering, *How did I make it here?* Despite my dire physical condition and back pain, I remained mentally alert.

During the year prior, 2004, while an inpatient and outpatient at St. John's Hospital, I was contacted by a counselor from the Senior Health Insurance Program of Illinois (SHIP). The counselor, a former nurse, was very helpful in coordinating my health care between retiree medical insurance and the hospital. She was very knowledgeable and caring. Thanks to her expert guidance, that aspect of my health care went very smoothly.

In 2005, while lying in bed at my sister's house waiting for the appointment at Northside for the

BMT program, I received a call from the SHIP counselor. I informed her that I had arrived safely and was waiting for my appointment, but she insisted that I phone the transplant group and alert them to the port (PICC line) in my arm. She said that immediate attention was necessary. The device was not malfunctioning but simply required regular maintenance and monitoring. I made the call and, as she had predicted, was instructed to immediately come to the facility.

When the nurse at Northside removed the bandages and saw the hole in the back of my neck, she left the room and another nurse came to examine the area. When the physician entered and examined me, he immediately admitted me to the hospital.

While hospitalized at Northside, I was visited by an infectious-disease doctor, an orthopedic surgeon, and a plastic surgeon. Each physician outlined the procedures that would follow. The orthopedic surgeon and the plastic surgeon focused on the cervical wound and the hardware. The infectious-disease doctor began preparations for antibiotic therapy for the staph infection, which was found to be methicillin-resistant. The rod was loose and infected.

The admitting physician decided that my condition was too critical at the time for a stem cell transplant. Given the severity of my condition, the procedure would be too risky. I just *knew* that I was in good hands. Later, I learned that he is a surgeon and a highly acclaimed medical expert in the field.

At the time, I was not concerned that the stem cell transplant was not going to proceed. However, several years later, after gathering information about the procedure, I was glad that it had not gone forward. I learned that the procedure is very delicate, using the patient's stem cells for the autologous transplant. Additionally, the patient might need a long-term caregiver to assist with meals, medications, and chores like grocery shopping. With all of that, the decision not to proceed at the time was obviously the best decision, especially with no guarantee of longevity.

After I was released from Northside Hospital and per the infectious-disease doctor's orders, I received home health care from a visiting nurses association. They administered clindamycin, gentamycin, and then vancomycin daily over a period of several months. IV therapy was used to administer the antibiotics.

In June 2005, at Saint Joseph's Hospital of Atlanta, the hardware was removed from the back of my neck. The orthopedic surgeon removed the rod, and the plastic surgeon removed skin from my right thigh and transferred it to the back of my neck to close the open area. The infectious-disease doctor steadily administered intravenous antibiotic treatment. Afterward, he prescribed a permanent daily dose of an antibiotic pill.

From hospital admittance to antibiotic therapy and the subsequent delicate and complicated hardware removal, this team of physicians was just superb. A friend had driven my car from Springfield to Atlanta. After the antibiotic therapy treatments were complete and the hardware was removed, I again attempted to turn the steering wheel. Amazingly, the steering wheel turned easily. My ability to turn the wheel felt normal again.

In June 2005, after the surgical procedures were accomplished and while I was still at my sister's house in Georgia, I settled into bone therapy treatments locally. I requested and received a referral for local oncological care from Northside Hospital. Not surprisingly, the oncologist was superb. The entire Georgia Cancer Specialists Group provided excellence in overall medical care.

My bone therapy treatments began at Georgia Cancer Specialists with the continuation of Aredia, which had been used in Springfield. Aredia (pamid-ronate disodium) is a member of a group of chemical compounds known as *bisphosphonates*, which slow the bone-destroying activity caused by multiple myeloma.[2] Aredia is available in 30 milligram or 90 milligram vials for intravenous administration.

Shortly afterward, the treatments were changed to Zometa. Zometa (zoledronic acid), in a 4 milligram injection, is a proven treatment that can help reduce and delay bone complications caused by cancer that has spread to the bone. Zometa, also in the class of bisphosphonates, works against the abnormal cells that cause the wearing away (or resorption) of bones.[3]

CHAPTER 3

Continued Oncology Care with Bone Therapy Treatments

In addition to excellent medical care, the support of family during critical times is very important. While remaining at my sister's house, I continued regularly scheduled bone therapy treatments at Georgia Cancer Specialists. The original plan was to have stem cell transplantation therapy and then return to Springfield. However, because of the change in itinerary, instead of returning to Springfield, I decided to remain in Atlanta to continue my cancer treatments.

After the intravenous antibiotic therapy and the removal of the rod from the top of my back at the

neck, I experienced signs of improvement. My pos-
ture improved, and my head gradually became more
comfortably erect, rather than sporadically falling
downward.

When I arrived in Atlanta with my sister earlier in 2005, my left foot was dragging and pointed
outward, in a slue-footed position. After the surgical
procedures and the antibiotic therapy, my left foot
once again pointed forward; hence, my stride improved. Also, as mentioned earlier, I had no problem
turning my car's steering wheel. Normality of a sort
was slowly returning as I gradually regained strength.

Settling into a routine with family members and
close friends, periodically, I walked for exercise. At
first, I walked slowly and only for a short distance,
and then gradually I increased both speed and distance. Of course, I had checked with one of my doctors, describing to him exactly what my walks consisted of and explaining that some locations were a
little hilly. He said it was okay as long as the inclines
were not steep.

For many years prior to the cancer diagnosis,
speed-walking and cycling had been my exercise
routine. I had also held health club memberships
and worked out regularly using the treadmill and

the walking track. I also participated in aerobic exercise classes. Walking continues to be a good form of exercise; however, with a condition such as mine, one must walk slowly and cautiously. Because of my extensive spinal surgeries, I no longer ride a bicycle or use the treadmill. Yet I continue to perform daily chores and run errands while paying attention to my limitations. I remain as active as my condition permits. The body lets one know its capabilities.

My condition dictates the level of speed at which I can comfortably and safely function; my capacity to perform daily activities; and my overall level of sustenance. Compare this to the way your body's reactions determine the amount of sleep that is necessary—whether more or less sleep is needed during the nighttime or a nap is needed during the day. Your body's reactions also let you know when too much or too little food has been consumed or whether you are carrying too much weight or too little. The key is to listen, pay attention, and respond accordingly.

My condition has resulted in a major lifestyle adjustment; however, I am very grateful to have life and the continued ability to function, even if it is much more slowly. I will add here that following doctors' orders and taking medications as prescribed are both very important. For example, recommendations to not consume alcohol while taking a particular medication should be strictly adhered to. Not even a glass of wine or a light beer is permitted, or even my favorite drink, a piña colada. Although I am only an occasional social drinker, since my cancer is terminal, I plan to never again consume an alcoholic beverage.

Additionally, if the label on a bottle of pills instructs the consumer to take a certain number at a specific time, then in order to receive the maximum benefit from the medication, I have learned that it is best to adhere strictly to that directive—no more and no less.

I always find it good to drink lots of water and maintain a healthy diet. The appropriate selection of foods depends on the medical condition.

CHAPTER 4

More Radiation Therapy and Chemotherapy Treatments

At the end of 2011, while handling my personal grocery cart, I made a swift motion with a twist that resulted in severe pain. The pain was so excruciating, I could barely walk. Since the pain was persistent, I was admitted to Saint Joseph's Hospital.

Radiation therapy treatments were administered at the hospital. After several weeks of outpatient radiation therapy, I received chemotherapy. The chemotherapy treatments were Velcade (bortezomib), an injection administered by a shot in the arm, and

Revlimid (lenalidomide), a capsule taken orally, used in conjunction with dexamethasone (a steroid).

Velcade, in a class of drugs called *proteasome inhibitors*, is used for the treatment of multiple myeloma and relapsed mantle cell lymphoma. The proteasomes break down proteins in both healthy and cancerous cells. As a targeted therapy, Velcade works to either block or slow the action of proteasomes inside cells.[4]

Revlimid is one of the innovative chemotherapy drugs used to treat multiple myeloma. A derivative of thalidomide, it is used along with dexamethasone. Revlimid targets specific proteins within cancer cells and stops the cancer cells from growing.[5]

Throughout 2012 and 2013, Revlimid was my monthly chemotherapy treatment along with weekly Velcade shots in the arm throughout 2012. Additionally, the monthly bone therapy treatments continued. Patient information concerning Revlimid usage warns of some serious possible side effects. Although I would feel extreme fatigue at times, the effects were relatively mild. In spite of the minor discomforts and to the extent possible, I continued functioning with day-to-day activities.

For the two-year period, and very effectively, CVS/ Caremark specialty pharmacy delivered the monthly

Revlimid capsules. As instructed, I took one capsule by mouth per day for twenty-one days of each twenty-eight day cycle; concurrently, I took dexamethasone once per week at ten pills of 4 milligrams each for a total of 40 milligrams per week.

Although very effective, my cancer treatments are expensive. Fortunately, during the first two critical years following my diagnosis, my retiree medical insurance was my primary coverage, and my health insurance covered medical and prescription drugs. However, with the advent of the 2005 Medicare Part D prescription drug program, Medicare Part D became my prescription drug coverage (per Medicare Part D Notice of Creditable Coverage).

From February 2006—two years after my cancer diagnosis, when my coverage was automatically switched from retiree medical to Medicare—through 2013, the coverage continued to be adequate. Medicare is the program that employers and employees fund through the FICA (Federal Insurance Contributions Act) tax. Medicare covers people age sixty-five and over and people under sixty-five with disabilities. Coverage begins either at age sixty-five or two years after a diagnosed illness that meets the criteria to qualify for social security disability.

Because Medicare coverage does not begin immediately upon becoming disabled, I was very fortunate that, upon receiving my cancer diagnosis, I was eligible for continued participation in my American Airlines Retiree Medical Plan, along with the AA Supplemental Medical Plan.

My cancer was in remission at year's end, 2013. During my two years of chemotherapy, the Medicare Part D plan adequately covered the cost of the Revlimid capsules. In fall of 2013, I received a notification of changes that were to begin in 2014. The providers give annual notification of price changes in prescription medications in October for the subsequent year beginning in January.

There were some variations in the levels of coverage. After several years of thorough and complete Medicare Part D coverage, in both brand-name and generic drugs, I experienced overall increased costs, co-pays, and fewer covered prescription drugs. Nevertheless, I am very grateful to have had the 2005 Medicare Part D prescription drug plan with such effective coverage throughout the two critical years of 2012 and 2013.

The substantial Social Security cost-of-living adjustments received through 2009 proved to be very helpful when I was faced with these additional prescription-drug costs. Specialty drugs can be very expensive. Throughout my medical journey, I am delighted to discover that there is lots of cooperation and patient support among providers, manufacturers, and retailers to ensure the patient's needs are met.

As they came after many years of frugality, the added costs to brand-name and generic drugs did not present a problem for me. However, due to the additional patient cost obligations overall, I advise anyone anticipating Medicare to maximize personal savings and investments to prepare for the possibility—particularly those who may anticipate extensive medical treatments. There are many legitimate savings and investment vehicles available.

After my oncologist at Georgia Cancer Specialists retired at the end of 2013, I continued bone therapy treatments there for a while. Then, in October 2014, I began treatments at the Winship Cancer Institute of Emory University. Dr. Jonathan Kaufman, doctor of hematology and medical oncology,[6] made several modifications to my ongoing cancer medications and treatments. Multiple myeloma is one of Dr. Kaufman's areas of specialization.

Not only am I extremely satisfied with the results

of the modifications he made, but I am equally content with the overall excellence in medical care at Emory. Considering the distance I have travelled with multiple myeloma and its consequences, my quality of life is very good. This is due to the quality medical providers and institutions.

Some have said my survival can also be attributed to my strength and determination, both physiological and psychological. Ultimately, my strength comes from a Higher Power, the One who sustains and guides me to the right places at the right times. That is, undeniably, my Lord and Savior, Jesus Christ.

Now that I have described the physical aspects of my journey, I will discuss what I strongly believe is the spiritual connection.

CHAPTER 5

The Spiritual Connection

Prior to the late seventies, if anyone had asked whether or not I believed in God, my answer would have been that I did not know. By definition, *agnostic*—not knowing yet not denying. However, during the latter part of that decade and beyond, when asked if I believed in God, I would have definitely, emphatically said yes! There is a valid reason why I confidently and doubtlessly secured that position. The knowledge was obtained experientially.

After my cancer diagnosis in 2004, I started a daily conversation with the Lord by citing two prayers from the Scriptures; first, Matthew 6:9-13 and then, Psalm 23:1-6. My relationship with the Lord has been a personal one.

When at times during my illness I have been asked how I did it—that is, sustained my ordeal—my answer has been twofold. Not only do I pray every day, but I also allow the Lord to lead me to the right people and places, and at the right times. I was always referred to medical providers and institutions just at the appropriate moment, which is characteristic of so much that has generally happened in my life.

Academically, at the graduate and undergraduate levels, my major course of study was philosophy. I chose philosophy because I found the curriculum to be interesting and stimulating. My goal was to obtain a bachelor's degree—although after receiving that degree, I continued on to complete a master of arts degree as well.

The philosophical school of thought I found to be most consistent with my belief was phenomenology, which is the science of phenomena.[7] Phenomena are facts or occurrences that can be perceived or observed.

Edmund Husserl (1859-1938), philosopher and mathematician, founded the twentieth-century philosophical school of phenomenology, illustrated in terms of pure phenomenology. According to Husserl, natural knowledge originates with experience; the sciences of experience are the sciences of *fact* (fact and essence).[8] Fact, that which is known to be objectively real, is determined by knowledge gained through experience; and I would add, that which is also verifiable through testing and experimentation.

In states of consciousness, as we know, that which is determined as fact is perceived by the five senses: sight, hearing, taste, smell, and touch. Pragmatically, as a general rule, I accept that which is ascertained by the five senses. However, expanding on Husserl's phenomenology, it is my opinion that another level of perception exists, one that is powered by an intense thought or feeling one might have about something. An example is a hunch or intuition, described as the capacity to know without the use of rational processes.[9]

Experience has shown me that, whether awake or in a state of sleep—sleep defined as a state of suspended consciousness[10]—one can acquire knowledge of something by paying attention to those intuitive feelings and/or by listening to those inner voices.

For example, I have at times experienced very vivid dreams—dreams so vivid it seems as though I am in an awakened state. On awakening, while proceeding with daily activities, I find myself moving in the same situation I had dreamed, whether on the subsequent day or much later. This occurred so frequently in the seventies that I determined that my dreams were not dreams but visions: the ability to see things before they occur. These experiences have been inspired most often by sight or by sound. With no universally accepted explanation for this abstract phenomenon, my description of it is to experience something that is already there.

I speculate that a hunch or intuition might be relative to a prior experience, possibly in the state of suspended consciousness: sleep. Perhaps this might provide some insight into the concept of déjà vu—a feeling of having already been there.

As a very organized person, I like to plan far in advance. However, in the process of decision-making, I frequently find myself overpowered by circumstances that lead to a result other than that which I have set as the ultimate goal.

This is exemplified by the simple act of arranging things at home and setting a goal to complete the task. On setting a goal for myself, although I feel certain that things are in order, an unexpected and overwhelming circumstance might occur that causes me to alter my plan, which as a consequence produces a different result. In the final analysis, I find myself more content with that which has resulted from the unexpected change.

When making plans or setting goals, I am very decisive and rigid. In regards to choosing a place to settle, for example, I lived in Evanston for many years with no plans of ever selling my home. However, in 2002, unforeseen circumstances unrelated to illness compelled me to sell and move from Evanston to Springfield. After resettling, I felt very content with the move. I expected the relocation to be difficult but instead, surprisingly, it went very smoothly.

Although the examples cited may seem trivial, the point is that when it comes to life in general, as I have experienced many times and over many years, a pattern of existence might already be laid out—preordained—and we therefore function within the parameters of this existence. This is evidenced in my experiences when, in spite of the paths that I chose, what the Lord had already determined for me was ultimately what would be—and, I will add, that which is always the best as well as the most desired result.

In 2004, a major unforeseen circumstance—my cancer diagnosis—compelled my eventual move to Atlanta. Although I had frequently visited the area for many years, I had no plans to actually relocate. On questioning myself as to why I did not contemplate the move many years earlier, I can only respond by accepting the consequences that led to the outcome and say that, in the final scheme of things, the Lord's plan was better than my plan.

I have concluded that life's discomforts are simply the necessities of the circumstances that lead to a designated place and time: fate. I have found it comforting to pay attention to those guiding inner thoughts and feelings. When resolving to take things as they are presented, absent of worry, I find that things flow smoothly and fall into place like the precut pieces of a jigsaw puzzle. I've learned that agonizing and worrying are futile wastes of time and effort, and I have come to know the inevitability of God's plan in every phase of my life.

Twelve years have now passed since I received my cancer diagnosis. My condition has vastly improved. I am feeling progressively better and in a good place. I must say that my ability to understand my survival on this journey with this complex cancer called multiple myeloma is contained within the truths of the Holy Bible, where I look for and always find verification and understanding.

CONCLUSION

A General Review

Cancer came suddenly after I had enjoyed a life-time of excellent health. There were few and un-recognizable signs. Multiple myeloma was unheard of by me until the diagnosis.

The ability to survive this terminal cancer compels me to share my experience with others. Although I am certainly not to be taken as an authority, I hope that sharing my experience gives hope and encouragement to anyone experiencing hopelessness and despair due to illness.

When one is diagnosed with a potentially devastating illness such as cancer, friends and family are important support systems. Gathering as many facts and as much information as possible about the illness can be helpful. When I was diagnosed with multiple myeloma, my sisters went online and found a wealth of information that enabled me to understand the cancer. It is good not only to stay active and continue functioning to the extent possible, but also to listen and learn. Listen to the medical experts and learn as much as possible about the condition.

Overall, quality medical care is important. Since cancer treatments can be very expensive, it is important to not only have adequate health insurance coverage but also a good, solid financial plan already in place to ready oneself for the potentiality of a serious, prolonged illness.

One's belief system is important. Since, in my opinion, there is order, purpose, design, and inevitability in all of life's occurrences, one must simply gather the strength to endure and possess the courage and determination to continue. That which sustains me is my firm belief—my ultimate trust in, and devotion to, God.

ABOUT THE AUTHOR

Presently, the author continues to reside in Georgia, in the vicinity of Atlanta, a large metropolis with lots of natural beauty—trees, blossoms, hills, sunshine, beautiful fall foliage, and a pleasant drive to the Atlantic Ocean. She is enjoying the climate, spending time with family and friends, and doing very well.

ENDNOTES

1 Kathy Giusti and Karen Andrews, "What Is Multiple Myeloma?" *The Multiple Myeloma Research Foundation*, 1998.

2 "A Visual Guide to Understanding Cancer," *Aredia Drug Information*, 2012, http://www.rxlist.com.

3 "The Backbone of Therapy for Bone Lesions," *Novartis Pharmaceuticals Corp.*, 2007.

4 "How Velcade (Bortezomib) Works," *Understanding Velcade*, 2014, http://www.velcade.com.

5 "Revlimid (Lenalidomide)," GoodRx, 2015, http://www.goodrx.com/revlimid.

6 Jonathan L. Kaufman, MD, Associate Professor and Associate Vice-Chair for Quality and Safety, Department of Hematology and Medical Oncology, Emory University School of Medicine; Medical Director and Section Chief, Ambulatory Infusion Centers, Winship Cancer Institute of Emory University, Atlanta.

7   Edmund Husserl, *Ideas: General Introduction to Pure Phenomenology*, translated by W.R. Boyce Gibson (New York/London: Collier Books/MacMillan, 1962).

8   Husserl.

9   *Webster's II New Riverside Dictionary* (Boston/New York: Houghton Mifflin Company, 1996).

10   *Webster's II.*

Lightning Source UK Ltd.
Milton Keynes UK
UKOW01f1602220218
318337UK00001B/2/P

Career
Teaching

SIXTH EDITION 30 ps

FELICITY TAYLOR

KOGAN PAGE
CAREERS
SERIES

First published in 1980
Sixth edition 1996

Kogan Page Limited
120 Pentonville Road
London N1 9JN

British Library Cataloguing in Publication Data

A CIP record for this book is available from the British Library

ISBN 0–7494–1819–2

Typeset by Kogan Page
Printed and bound in Great Britain by Clays Ltd, St Ives plc

Contents

Part 1: What is Teaching Like?

Introduction   **9**
How To Use This Book 9

1. **What Teaching is About**   **11**
Education Law 11; What Sort of People Become
Teachers? 12; Appraisal 14; Inspection 15; How
Long is the Working Day? 15; Employment
Prospects 16

2. **The Career Structure**   **20**
Teachers' Salaries 20; Conditions of Employment
22; What Does This Mean in Practice? 33; Posts of
Responsibility 35; Induction and In-Service
Training 36

3. **Finding a Job**   **38**
How to Apply 38; Preparing for the Interview 39;
Conditions of Employment 40; Teachers' Unions 42;
Other Openings for Qualified Teachers 42

Part 2: How to Qualify as a Teacher

Introduction   **47**

4. **Teaching Qualifications**   **49**
England and Wales 49; Scotland 54; Northern
Ireland 57

5. **Where to Study**   **58**
    Choosing a Course 58; Choosing a College 59;
    Mature Students 60; Licensed Teachers Scheme 60;
    Students with Disabilities 60; Specialist Subjects:
    Art and Design, Drama 62; Teaching Children with
    Special Needs 63; Special Qualifications 64

6. **How to Apply**   **66**
    University Degree Courses 66; Teacher Education
    Courses at Colleges and Institutions of Higher
    Education, Universities and Colleges of Education
    67; Postgraduate Certificate of Education (PGCE)
    Courses 69; Interviews 70; Student Grants 71;
    Grants for DipHE Students 71; How to Apply for
    Grants 72

7. **Training Courses**   **74**
    Colleges Offering Initial Teacher Training 74;
    University Degree Courses with an Education
    Content 80; Postgraduate Certificate of Education
    (PGCE) Courses 82; The Open University 89

8. **Further Reading**   **91**
    Higher Education 91; Teacher Training Agency 92;
    General 92; National Press 92

9. **Useful Addresses**   **93**

Part 1:
What is Teaching Like?

Introduction

Teachers can make a difference. The wave of criticism of the profession a few years ago, however unfair, was in itself a recognition of just how important teachers are. That is one of the reasons why there are still so many teachers who say that they love their job and could not imagine doing anything else.

At least no one can say that a teacher's life is dull. Every child and every class offers a different challenge, especially in the freer climate of contemporary teaching.

So do not be put off by the accounts of teacher disillusionment and low morale. Far more important to most teachers is meeting the challenge of the classroom and reaping the very real reward of seeing their pupils conquer difficulties, widen their understanding and make often astonishing progress. Schools need the best teachers they can get, and there is no doubt that people coming out of the colleges nowadays are better trained than ever before.

As a recent government publication on teaching as a career put it, 'Teaching has changed. In the last few years, new perspectives, new objectives and new ideas have all been playing their part in shaping the management of that change, injecting a new dynamism and giving new zest to a career which, for the right people, has the potential to be one of the most satisfying and worthwhile to be found.'

How to Use This Book

The book is in two parts. Part 1 gives you general information about school teaching as a career, what sort of people become teachers, what the prospects are for promotion and what it is like to be a teacher, including case studies of qualified teachers. Part 2 gives details about the qualifications you will need to become a teacher and the many different ways there are of obtaining them.

Although you may not want to commit yourself to a teaching career as soon as you leave school for higher education, it is a good idea to know what the possibilities are and to make sure that you are not disqualifying yourself from teaching by the subjects you choose to study or the courses you choose to take. In fact, this process begins as early as year 9 in secondary school when you make decisions about your Key Stage 4 course. Anyone who wants to take up teaching needs to have GCSEs or their equivalent in English language and maths.

This book can give you only a general guide to teaching as a career. You should also ask for help from your careers advisers and your school and parents in making up your mind. In addition you will need specific information from the college prospectuses and course guides.

Chapter 1

What Teaching is About

Education Law

The last seven years have seen dramatic changes in the education system. The 1988 Education Act set up Local Management of Schools (LMS). Governors were made responsible for deciding how the budget delegated to the school by the LEA was spent, including numbers of staff; their selection and appointment; pay policies, grievance and discipline procedures. This Act established the National Curriculum (NC) and a system of testing of pupils at four Key Stages. Governors have to ensure that the National Curriculum is implemented in their schools and that the curriculum is broad and balanced and includes religious education. The Act also introduced Grant Maintained Schools (GMS) which opt out of LEA control. The 1992 Education Act changed the inspection of schools, setting up OFSTED (Office for Standards in Education) to administer a system of four-yearly inspections of all schools by teams of inspectors (including at least one lay inspector) under contract to OFSTED.

The 1992 Further and Higher Education Act made colleges for students over 16, including sixth-form colleges, independent corporations, no longer controlled by local education authorities. This Act also set up a Higher Education Funding Council to fund universities and other higher education colleges and allowed all approved institutions to use the name 'University'.

The 1993 Education Act set up the School Curriculum and Assessment Authority (SCAA). Among other provisions the Secretary of State can appoint Education Associations to take over the management of schools deemed to be failing. The Act strengthens the law on special educational needs so as to improve parents' rights.

Every school in England and Wales supported by public funds has a governing body. This includes elected parent and teacher governors, representatives of the local community and, in voluntary-aided, often church schools, foundation governors nominated by the body that originally set up the school. There is a similar system in Northern Ireland. In Scotland there is a system of School Boards with more limited powers.

The Teacher's Duty of Care

Because parents have to send their children to school, teachers have to take on a heavy responsibility for the children in their care. As long as the children are legally in their charge, teachers must take the same care of them all as a reasonable and careful parent would. On a school journey or visit this means responsibility for the whole time the children are away from home. Although the standard is that of *reasonable care,* recent tragic events on school journeys have demonstrated just how high that standard has to be, and what a great deal society expects from its teachers.

The teaching unions can provide advice and support in legal matters for their members (see page 42).

What Sort of People Become Teachers?

The short answer, as anyone who has been in the staffroom of a large comprehensive school will tell you, is all sorts. They do, of course, tend to be people who have done well enough at school to stay on into the sixth form or go on to further education. This in turn means that there is a higher proportion of entrants from what the sociologists call the ABC groups of the population, because it is these more prosperous groups that still produce most of the students in higher education. However, teaching has always been one of the professions most open to students from working-class families. There tend to be more women teachers than men because teaching young children has in the past been thought of as a woman's job, though this is at last beginning to change. One interesting point is that a very much higher proportion of student teachers than you would expect have either one or both parents in the teaching profession. So their experiences cannot have been all bad.

In spite of some of the stereotypes in the popular press, teachers hold all kinds of political views. People specialising in arts subjects are more likely to want to become teachers than those qualifying in science or technical subjects. When asked why they chose teaching, student teachers stressed the importance of working with people, helping others and forming good personal relationships. They rated these aspects of a career more highly than attributes such as financial reward, efficiency or economic relevance.

Obviously, you need to be the kind of person who gets on well with other people. This does not mean that it is essential to be a lively extrovert, but it will make your life as a teacher much more comfortable if you find it easy to make friends in the staffroom as well as with children and their parents. You also need to like children. That sounds like a truism, though many pupils can tell you about teachers who appear to be lacking in this particular quality. It is not always easy to know whether this means you. Some people make up their minds very early on that they want to teach. Probably most young people have thought of it seriously at one time or another, perhaps because they themselves were doing well at school, or even because they were unhappy at school and felt that they could prevent that happening to others. On the other hand, a typical case is that of a student in her last year at university, with no idea of what she wanted to do afterwards, who was taken by chance on a visit to an infant school in the area. She was so impressed by the work she saw going on there that she immediately decided to apply for teacher training, although she had never thought of it before!

You should get plenty of opportunities at school to find out how you get on with children, whether or not you come from a large family yourself. Most schools put some form of community education and service on the timetable, and you will be able to go out into playgroups and primary schools, helping with the younger children and seeing what it is like to be with them and responsible for them all day long. Even if this is not available at your school, you can help with playgroups and youth groups in your free time.

Holiday activities for children always need young people, perhaps as volunteers to help with holidays for children with special needs, or as paid workers on the many children's holidays you see advertised in the press.

When you apply for a teacher education course you will be asked to show that you have observed pupils of the age you wish to teach in school. Do you enjoy helping with the younger classes at your school? Do you get impatient when they are slow to understand what you are trying to show them? Do they take any notice when you tell them what to do?

One of the problems of deciding whether someone would be a good teacher is the difficulty of describing what a good teacher is like. We think we know whether a teacher is good or bad, but when it comes to setting out their characteristics objectively it is much more difficult to agree. In a paper entitled 'Partners in Change', Michael Barber and Tim Brighouse set out some of the qualities and skills that good teachers should aspire to. Their list included:

☐ Good understanding of self
☐ Generosity of spirit
☐ Sharp observational powers
☐ Interest in and concern for others
☐ Infectious enthusiasm for what is taught
☐ Imagination
☐ Energy
☐ Intellectual curiosity.

You could also add good team players, willingness to share ideas and good practice; tolerance; not being afraid of making mistakes and profiting from them, allowing children that facility. But we all know good teachers who would not fit any criteria. Perhaps the easiest way out is to say that after all, teachers are people too, and come in all shapes and sizes. It does help, though, to be reasonably organised in your daily life.

Appraisal

All teachers now have to be appraised regularly on a two-year cycle. The LEA or the governing body of a grant-maintained school is the body responsible for managing the appraisal system, but most appraisals will be carried out in school by the head and senior management.

It is important to see appraisal as an essential part of staff and career development, working with teachers to help them to raise educational standards. Teachers should be fully involved in the planning process and in the targets set during appraisal, which should also relate to the priorities set by the school development plan.

Inspection

Under the OFSTED inspection arrangements every school is to be inspected at least once every four years. The main focus of the inspection is on the quality of teaching and learning – in other words on what is going on in the classroom. Teachers are expected to have clear lesson plans related to their written schemes of work. Many schools have been criticised for having expectations of their pupils that were too low.

How Long is the Working Day?

Just as bank clerks suffer from the popular belief that they only work when the banks are open, so people tend to think that teachers work a five-hour day for half the year. Just how long a teacher's day is has been a matter for bitter contention for the last few years, but it can safely be said that averagely conscientious teachers would normally expect to spend at least half as much time preparing and marking work as they do in front of a class. Then consider the time spent on out-of-school activities, parent-teacher meetings and in-service training courses, and you begin to get the teacher's 'easy' life in perspective. Ask any mother what it would be like to have sole charge of and responsibility for 30 young children for a whole morning and a whole afternoon five days a week, with a short break for lunch if you are lucky and a cup of coffee at playtime if you are not on duty. Secondary school teachers may get some free periods according to their responsibilities, but they have to cope with the demands of facing a different class every 40 or 80 minutes. However, there is no doubt that the hours and holidays are a valuable incentive, especially for working mothers or women who intend to become working mothers some time in the future.

The contract of employment for teachers is discussed in Chapter 2.

Employment Prospects

The rapid decline in the birth rate which has had such a dramatic effect on schools has come to an end. The numbers of pupils in both primary and secondary schools are now expected to rise steadily for the next five to ten years. Like all public spending, education finance has been strictly controlled but it seems probable that education will be treated rather more favourably in the next few years. This would certainly be popular among parents and governors as well as teachers.

The Department for Education and Employment (DFEE) tries to keep the number of teacher training places in balance with the estimated demand. In 1995 there were about 14,000 places on secondary courses and about 16,000 for primary teaching. The School Teachers' Pay Review Body keeps a careful eye on recruitment and retention of staff. Its 1995 report concluded that the supply and demand for teachers was in balance at that time but needed continuing attention to make sure that the quality of teachers remained high.

Shortage Subjects

Even when there are large numbers of students applying to take teacher training courses there is still a shortage of teachers in certain subjects. The DFEE offers a range of incentives to recruit more specialists into these areas.

For a number of years the DFEE has provided a bursary scheme through which graduates training to teach maths, physics, balanced science, chemistry, technology, craft, design and technology, modern foreign languages and Welsh, may be eligible for a tax-free bursary of £1000 a year. This was for full-time students only and was in addition to the normal student grant. Most students accepted on a full-time Postgraduate Certificate of Education (PGCE) course or one of the specially shortened BEd courses to teach these subjects were eligible, as long as they intended to teach in a maintained school.

From 1996–97 the Teacher Training Agency are setting up a Priority Recruitment Scheme to replace the current bursary scheme. It will cover similar subjects with the addition of religious education. Instead of a national scheme colleges will be invited to apply for funds to run their own schemes, which could include recruitment activities as well as support for individual students.

Full details can be obtained from careers advisers or from the Teacher Training Agency (TTA).

If students have not obtained the right qualifications at school, some colleges will provide conversion courses to give the necessary basic knowledge. Requirements for GCSE qualifications may be relaxed for some courses.

The problem is not so acute in Scotland, perhaps because of the wider base of sixth-form studies in Scottish schools.

Case Studies

Nikki is a 26-year-old teacher in charge of the sixth form at an inner city comprehensive.

I remember when I was 17 our sixth-form teacher told me I would make a marvellous teacher and I was horrified. I was very anti-establishment in those days and teaching was the last thing I wanted to do. Yet in my third year at university I had no plans for a job, so I thought I might as well take the teacher training certificate. After that year I went back to college to do an MA and then decided that I would like to teach in a further education college. But when I went for the interview they told me to get some school experience first, so I went to work in a school, thinking it would be for just a couple of years.

However, once I was working in a school I got more and more involved. I know it sounds big-headed, but I began to realise how much schools needed people who were committed and had something to offer. And in my second year of teaching I was made a sixth-form tutor, which was lucky as it gave me the chance to work with older pupils.

Teaching is a curious business. One of the odd and rather worrying things about it is the tremendous amount of power and responsibility the individual teacher has. There are rules about professional behaviour, but when you are alone with 20 children in a classroom it's up to you. You have almost total autonomy. The influence you can have over the kids, though far less powerful than you think it is, is both alarming and stimulating. You influence them by force of personality, and then you go away and it seems to wear off. Later you see them again and realise that at least some of what you were trying to put over has stuck.

Another of the dangerously attractive things about teaching is the self-satisfaction and self-righteousness it encourages. Everyone tells you that you are a saint, that you don't get paid enough, so you feel it is a job many people couldn't or wouldn't do. And when I compare my work with some of my contemporaries in other professions, in terms of responsibilities and job satisfaction, I get an awful lot more than they do, although the salary may be lower. Of course, I am lucky to have a senior post and lots of new responsibilities, but I liked it before that. I get frustrated with the admin and all the obvious difficulties but I love being with kids.

I was talking with some college students on teaching practice and our sixth form about what makes a good teacher. The sixth-formers all said that the most important thing was for the teacher to be very involved. It is the kind of job that is never finished; there is always something more you could do, although there are plenty of people who get by on shutting up shop at 4 pm and all through the holidays. A friend of mine told me the other day that I was becoming a workaholic, neglecting other areas of my life. Teaching is a big act, and I sometimes wonder if the act is taking over and where am I?

Another thing you must have is physical stamina. I was taking a discussion group which the students were in and for a solid hour I was on my feet directing the conversation of 25 lively people. The students said afterwards that just watching had made them feel exhausted. It is difficult to keep that up for five hours a day, five days a week, though you ought to. Perhaps teaching is a profession that you work in for only five years at a time and then go off and do something else. And yet when I think of doing some other job, I can't imagine one that would give me the same satisfaction. It has increased my self-confidence enormously, learning how to cope with large numbers of people. I went into teaching for the wrong reasons, in a rather haphazard way, but I've found my vocation.

Siobhan is a student on a Postgraduate Certificate of Education course.

My parents are both teachers and so is my brother, so I swore I wouldn't be one. I resisted for three and a half years. I worked in administrative jobs in health and housing and I found that the educational side of the work was what really interested me, so I had to give in. What I enjoy most is not the course, but being with the children. It gives me the chance to explore and develop my character and personality in ways you can't find in an administrative job. Teaching is not just intellectual, it's very intuitive; you have to give quick responses, and I find I enjoy that.

I'm training to teach junior children and I find it very stimulating to teach right across the curriculum – maths and science as well as the English I took my degree in. I get very depressed by the effects of the education cuts. There is so much going on as far as the curriculum is concerned, new experiments, a lot of concern about the best way to teach and make things better, and all this is being hampered by the cuts and the pressure on teachers.

Student teachers at a school can be in a very vulnerable position – more or less uninvited guests. There are aspects of the régime in the school where I am doing my teaching practice that I would certainly want to try to change if I were on the staff but, of course, as a student I can't. It is insane that the PGCE course lasts only eight months. If you get through it is something in *you*, not in the course. I think older people who have had some time away from college are at an advantage here.

But all the students in my group are still enthusiastic, in spite of everything.

Mike teaches in a suburban primary school.

I teach a Year 6 class of 32 nine-year-olds and I am also the maths co-ordinator for the junior school. I enjoy my work enormously, because the children are such a good age to teach. They are still excited by learning and not too spoiled by television and other outside pressures. My big problem, like everyone else these days, is not enough time. But now that I have learned to use a computer to help with a lot of the routine record-keeping, it is not so bad. The worst time is doing the end of year reports. In May this year I did about three A4 pages on each of my 32 pupils, and by the end it was getting rather difficult to think of something original to say. But it is worth it when parents come in and are so obviously pleased and grateful that you have shown that you really know their child.

The worst thing for teachers, I find, is when you can't get support from the parents. We have this joint reading scheme, parents, teachers and children working together, so that parents can read with their child at home. But there are always one or two who won't co-operate and it is the children who really need support that seem to miss out.

Chapter 2

The Career Structure

The pay and career structure of teachers in England and Wales is decided nationally according to the Teachers' Pay and Conditions Act 1991. In Scotland, the Scottish Teachers' Salaries Committee regulates teaching salaries. Although schools in the independent sector can in theory pay what they like, in practice their salaries are geared to the national scales and they tend to rely on smaller classes and longer holidays to attract staff. Grant-maintained schools are bound by the Teachers' Pay Regulations unless they have obtained an exemption from the Secretary of State.

Each year a Teachers' Pay and Conditions Document based on the findings of the Pay Review Committee is issued setting out pay scales and other conditions for that year. Most schools or large reference libraries should have a copy of the current document, or it is obtainable from HMSO.

Teachers' Salaries

The Act specifies one scale for all teachers except heads and deputies. Heads and deputies are paid on a pay spine divided according to the 'group' the school belongs to, which depends on the number and ages of the pupils.

For 1996–97, teachers are paid on a single 18-point pay spine. Points can be given under six headings, some mandatory, others discretionary.

Qualifications
Two points must be given for a good honours degree or equivalent.

Experience
One point for each year of satisfactory service, up to a maximum of seven points (or nine points for those without a good degree). This is known as incremental progression, and is an entitlement unless the teacher's performance has been demonstrably unsatisfactory that year. Governors then have the power to withhold the spine point. A teacher deemed unsatisfactory must be warned in advance, given help to improve, and has the right of appeal. The point may be restored at a later date.

Additional points may be given for appropriate experience outside teaching. Experience points cannot be withdrawn even if the teacher moves to another post.

Responsibilities
Up to five points may be given for extra responsibilities 'beyond those common to the majority of teachers'. Responsibility points may be given temporarily for temporary extra duties, otherwise teachers keep them while they remain in the same post. People with similar responsibilities should get similar points.

Excellence
Up to three points may be awarded for excellent performance, particularly in classroom teaching. All teachers are eligible and the award of points comes up for renewal each year and may be withdrawn. Governors should carefully consider the effect on future funding and staff morale, and the practical difficulties of establishing clearly measurable criteria.

Recruitment and Retention
Up to two points (three in inner London) may be given for shortage subjects or posts hard to fill. These must be reviewed every two years.

Special Educational Needs
All teachers working mainly with children with statements of special educational need must receive one point. One point may be given to a teacher who mainly teaches pupils with special needs who do not all have statements. A second point may be given for special qualifications or experience and expertise in the field of special needs.

So you can see that within the national guidelines there is a wide range of options about what teachers should be paid, and many opportunities for rewarding teachers who have outstanding skills. The problem is to identify these without causing ill-will.

Unqualified teachers may not be employed unless there is no alternative. They are paid on a special scale. Part-time teachers are paid a proportion of the appropriate annual rate. Licensed teachers may be paid either as qualified teachers in which case they are eligible for allowances, or as unqualified teachers.

Heads and deputies do not receive annual increments, though the range of salaries may increase each year. Governing bodies have discretion to choose at what point on the pay spine they will pay their heads and deputies, within the guidelines for the size of school. They can exceed those guidelines if they feel that their school's circumstances warrant this. They can also set performance targets for heads that trigger pay rises.

In 1995–96 the main scale begins at £11,883 rising to £32,169. Teachers serving in the London area get an inner, outer or fringe area London allowance to compensate for the extra cost of living. The pay spine for heads and deputy heads starts at £23,676 with a top figure of £53,559 for the largest schools. Some governing bodies also offer a package of fringe benefits to attract high quality applicants for headship and governors can pay above the scale if they feel it is necessary to recruit the right person.

Conditions of Employment

The Act also specified conditions of service which must be incorporated into teachers' contracts of employment. Detailed provisions about teachers' hours and duties form part of their legal contract with their employers and the responsibility to do more than just teach in front of a class is specified.

Teachers
Reproduced below are relevant extracts from the Order, approved by Parliament. These apply to teachers other than head teachers.

Exercise of General Professional Duties
1. A teacher who is not a head teacher shall carry out the

professional duties of a school teacher as circumstances may require:

(a) if he is employed as a teacher in a school, under the reasonable direction of the head teacher of that school;

(b) if he is employed by an authority on terms under which he is not assigned to any one school, under the reasonable direction of that authority and of the head teacher of any school in which he may for the time being be required to work as a teacher.

Exercise of Particular Duties

2. (a) A teacher employed as a teacher (other than a head teacher) in a school shall perform, in accordance with any directions which may reasonably be given to him by the head teacher from time to time, such particular duties as may reasonably be assigned to him.

(b) A teacher employed by an authority on terms such as those described in paragraph 1(b) above shall perform, in accordance with any direction which may reasonably be given to him from time to time by the authority or by the head teacher of any school in which he may for the time being be required to work as a teacher, such particular duties as may reasonably be assigned to him.

Professional Duties

3. The following duties shall be deemed to be included in the professional duties which a school teacher may be required to perform:

Teaching	(1)	(a)	Planning and preparing courses and lessons.
		(b)	Teaching, according to their educational needs, the pupils assigned to him, including the setting and marking of work to be carried out by the pupil in school and elsewhere.
		(c)	Assessing, recording and reporting on the development, progress and attainment of pupils.
Other activities	(2)	(a)	Promoting the general progress and

well-being of individual pupils and of any class or group of pupils assigned to him.

(b) Providing guidance and advice to pupils on educational and social matters and on their further educational and future careers including information about sources of more expert advice on specific questions; making relevant records and reports.

(c) Making records of and reports on the personal and social needs of pupils.

(d) Communicating and consulting with the parents of pupils.

(e) Communicating and co-operating with persons or bodies outside the school.

(f) Participating in meetings arranged for any of the purposes described above.

Assessments and reports (3) Providing or contributing to oral and written assessments, reports and references relating to individual pupils and groups of pupils.

Appraisal (4) Participating in any arrangements within an agreed national framework for the appraisal of his performance and that of other teachers.

Review: Further training and development (5) (a) Reviewing from time to time his methods of teaching and programmes of work.

(b) Participating in arrangements for his further training and professional development as a teacher.

Educational methods (6) Advising and co-operating with the head teacher and other teachers (or any one or more of them) on the preparation and development of courses of study, teaching materials, teaching programmes, methods of teaching and assessment and pastoral arrangements.

Discipline, health and safety	(7)	Maintaining good order and discipline among pupils and safeguarding their health and safety.

Staff meetings (8) Participating in meetings at the school which relate to the curriculum for the school or the administration or organisation of the school, including pastoral arrangements.

Cover (9) Supervising and so far as practicable teaching any pupils whose teacher is absent:

Provided that no teacher shall be required to provide such cover –

(a) after the teacher who is absent has been absent for three or more consecutive working days; or

(b) where the fact that the teacher would be absent for a period exceeding three consecutive working days was known to the maintaining authority no less than two working days before the absence commenced,

unless –

(i) he is a teacher employed wholly or mainly for the purpose of providing such cover (a 'supply teacher'); or

(ii) the services of a supply teacher to provide cover for the absent teacher are not available; or

(iii) the teacher required to provide cover is a full-time teacher at the school but has been assigned by the head teacher in the timetable to teach or carry out other specified duties (except cover) for less than 75 per cent of the hours covered by the school timetable.

Public examinations (10) Participating in arrangements for preparing pupils for public examinations and in assessing pupils for the purpose of such examinations; recording and reporting such assessments; participating in arrangements for pupils' presentation for and supervision during such examinations.

Selection etc of staff   (11)   Contributing to the selection for appointment and professional development of other teachers, including the assessment of probationary teachers.

Management   (12)   (a)   Co-ordinating or managing the work of other teachers.

(b)   Taking such part as may be required of him in the review, development and management of activities relating to the curriculum, organisation and pastoral functions of the school.

Administration   (13)   (a)   Participating in administrative and organisational tasks related to such duties as are described above, including the management or supervision of persons providing support for the teachers in the school and the ordering and allocation of equipment and materials.

(b)   Attending assemblies, registering the attendance of pupils and supervising pupils, whether these duties are to be performed before, during or after school sessions.

Working Time

(1)   A teacher employed full-time, other than in the circumstances described in Paragraph 3, shall be available for work for 195 days in any school year, of which 190 days shall be days on which he or she may be required to teach pupils in addition to carrying out other duties; and those 195 days shall be specified by his employer or, if the employer so directs, by the head.

(2)   Such a teacher shall be available to perform such duties at such times and such places as may be specified by the

head for 1,265 hours in any school year, to be allocated reasonably throughout those days on which he or she is required to work.

(3)   subparagraphs (1) and (2) do not apply to a teacher employed to teach or perform other duties in relation to pupils in a residential establishment;

(4)   time spent in travelling to or from the place of work shall not count against the 1,265 hours referred to in subparagraph (1);

(5)   unless employed under a separate contract as a midday supervisor, a teacher shall not be required to undertake midday supervision, and shall be allowed a break of reasonable length either between school sessions or between the hours of 12 noon and 2 pm;

(6)   a teacher shall, in addition to the requirements set out in subparagraphs (1) and (2) above, work such additional hours as may be needed to enable him to discharge effectively his professional duties, including in particular the marking of pupils' work and the preparation of lessons, teaching material and teaching programmes. The amount of time required for this purpose beyond the 1,265 specified hours referred to in subparagraph (2) and the times outside the 1,265 specified hours at which duties shall be performed shall not be defined by the employer but shall depend upon the work needed to discharge the teacher's duties.

Head Teachers
Reproduced overleaf are relevant extracts from the Order.

Overriding
requirements

(1)   A head teacher shall carry out his
professional duties in accordance with
and subject to –

(a)   the provisions of the Education Acts
1944 to 1993;

(b)   any orders and regulations having
effect thereunder;

(c)   the articles of government of the
school of which he is head teacher, to
the extent to which their content is
prescribed by statute;

(d)   where the school is a voluntary school
or a grant-maintained school which
was formerly a voluntary school any
trust deed;

(e)   any scheme of local management;

and, as long as they are not
inconsistent with the law and
regulations, to rules, regulations and
policies laid down by his or her
employers; the terms of his or her
appointment.

Consultation

In carrying out his duties he shall consult,
where this is appropriate, with the authority,
the governing body, the staff of the school,
and the parents of its pupils.

Professional
duties
School aims

The professional duties of a head teacher
shall include –

(1)   Formulating the overall aims and
objectives of the school and policies for
their implementation.

Appointment of
staff

(2)   Participating in the selection and
appointment of the staff of the school.

Management

(3)   (a) Deploying and managing all
teaching and non-teaching staff of
the school and allocating
particular duties to them
(including such duties of the head
teacher as may properly be
delegated to the deputy head
teacher or other members of the

staff), in a manner consistent with their conditions of employment, maintaining a reasonable balance for each teacher between work carried out in school and work carried out elsewhere.

(b) Considering, in particular in relation to such allocation of duties, how far the duties of the head may be delegated to any deputy head.

(c) Ensuring that the duty of providing cover for absent teachers, as prescribed in paragraph 3(9) of Schedule 3, is shared equitably among all teachers in the school, taking account of their teaching and other duties.

(d) Ensuring that teachers at the school receive information they need in order to carry out their professional duties effectively.

General functions

Subject to the above, a head shall be responsible for the internal organisation, management and control of the school.

Liaison with staff unions and associations

(4) Maintaining relationships with organisations representing teachers and other persons on the staff of the school.

Curriculum

(5) (a) Determining, organising and implementing an appropriate curriculum for the school, having regard to the needs, experience, interests, aptitudes and stage of development of the pupils and the resources available to the school.

(b) Securing that all pupils at the school take part in daily collective worship.

Review	(6)	Keeping under review the work and organisation of the school.
Standards of teaching and learning	(7)	Evaluating the standards of teaching and learning in the school, and ensuring that proper standards of professional performance are established and maintained.
Appraisal of staff	(8)	(a) Supervising and participating in arrangements for the appraisal of the performance of teachers in the school, participating in arrangements made for the appraisal of his or her performance as head, and that of other heads; participating in the identification of areas in which he or she would benefit from further training and undergoing such training.
Training and development of staff		(b) Ensuring that all staff in the school have access to advice and training appropriate to their needs, in accordance with the policies of the maintaining authority for the development of staff.
		(c) Ensuring that newly qualified teachers and those returning to teaching have access to adequate support during their first year of service.
Management information	(9)	Providing information about the work and performance of the staff employed at the school where this is relevant to their future employment.
Pupil progress	(10)	Ensuring that the progress of the pupils of the school is monitored and recorded.
Pastoral care	(11)	Determining and ensuring the implementation of a policy for the pastoral care of the pupils.

Discipline

(12) (a) Determining, in accordance with any written statement of general principles provided for him by the governing body, measures to be taken with a view to promoting, among the pupils, self-discipline and proper regard for authority, encouraging good behaviour on the part of the pupils, ensuring that the standard of behaviour of the pupils is acceptable, and otherwise regulating the conduct of the pupils; making such measures generally known within the school and ensuring that they are implemented.

(b) Ensuring the maintenance of good order and discipline on the school premises whenever pupils are present, including the midday break and wherever pupils are engaged in authorised school activities on the premises or elsewhere.

Relations with parents

(13) Making arrangements for parents to be consulted and given regular information about the school curriculum, the progress of their children and other matters affecting the school, so as to promote common understanding of its aims.

Relations with other bodies

(14) Promoting effective relationships with persons and bodies outside the school.

Relations with governing body

(15) Advising and assisting the governing body of the school in the exercise of its functions, including (without prejudice to any rights he may have as a governor of the school) attending meetings of the governing body and making such reports to it in connection with the discharge of his functions as it may properly require either on a regular basis or from time to time.

Relations with authority	(16)	Maintaining liaison and ensuring co-operation with the officers of the maintaining authority: making such reports to the authority in connection with the discharge of his functions as it may properly require either on a regular basis or from time to time.
Relations with other educational establishments	(17)	Maintaining liaison with other schools and further education establishments with which the school has a relationship.
Resources	(18)	Allocating, controlling and accounting for those financial and material resources of the school which are under the control of the head teacher.
Premises	(19)	Making provision, if so required by the governing body or the maintaining authority, for the security and effective supervision of the school buildings and their contents and of the school grounds; ensuring (if so required) that any lack of maintenance is promptly reported to the maintaining authority or, if appropriate, the governing body.
Absence	(20)	Arranging for a deputy head teacher or other suitable person to assume responsibility for the discharge of his functions as head teacher at any time when he is absent from school.
Teaching	(21)	Participating to such extent as may be appropriate in the teaching of the pupils of the school.
Daily break		A head teacher shall be allowed a break of reasonable length in the course of each school day, and should arrange for a suitable person to assume responsibility during that break.

Deputy Head Teachers
Reproduced below is a relevant extract from the Order.

General duties

A person appointed deputy head teacher in a school, in addition to carrying out the professional duties of a school teacher, including those duties particularly assigned to him by the head teacher, shall –

(1) play a major role under the overall direction of the head in

(a) formulating the aims and objectives of the school;

(b) establishing the policies through which they are achieved;

(c) managing staff and resources to that end;

(d) monitoring progress towards their achievement;

(2) undertake any professional duty of the head teacher which may reasonably be delegated to him by the head teacher;

(3) undertake, in the absence of the head teacher and to the extent required by him or his employers, the professional duties of the head teacher;

(4) be entitled to a break of reasonable length as near to the middle of each school day as is reasonably practicable.

Note. The conditions of employment of deputy head teachers would also include the conditions applying to ordinary teachers.

What Does This Mean in Practice?

Teachers have always accepted that they had obligations beyond formal lessons. The difficulty lies in defining just what these extra duties should be, and in fact there is an escape clause in the contract where it says that teachers must work extra hours beyond the 1,265 specified, if this is necessary to discharge their professional duties effectively. The many very conscientious teachers will continue to put in long hours outside school on preparation, marking and extra-curricular activities, because they find this personally satisfying, regardless of any legislation.

Posts of responsibility mean different things in different

schools. In a small primary school, a teacher might get an extra point for responsibility for the library, or for language development throughout the school. In a large comprehensive school, heads of large departments might get four extra points. Heads of House or heads of Year, with pastoral responsibilities for a large group of pupils, would also qualify for several additional points. In a smaller school, or in a small subject department, the head of that department might get two points.

Here is the kind of structure you might find in a large mixed county comprehensive school:

Staffing Structure

Head
Deputy head
Senior teacher. 5 points.

4 points
Four heads of faculty – Science, Maths, Humanities, Special Needs

2 points
Six heads of Year
Director of Music
Heads of Language, Information Technology, Technology, Physical Education, Personal, Social and Moral Education (PSME), Modern Languages, Creative Arts, Business Studies, Pre-vocational Education
Deputy head of Science
Deputy head of Maths
Deputy head Special Needs

1 extra point
Six deputy heads of Year (also have curricular responsibilities)
Deputy head Modern Languages
Deputy head Art
Deputy head PE

Main scale posts
Maths (2)
Science (2)
English (2)
English as a Second Language (1)

History/Geography (2)
French/Spanish (1)
Music (1)
Technology (2)
Home Economics (1)

Another example:

Primary School, Junior Mixed and Infants: 220 on roll

Staff Employed
Head
Deputy head – responsible for language throughout the school

Post with 2 additional points
1. Responsibility for reception arrangements; infants; liaison with local playgroups.
2. Language co-ordinator.
3. Maths co-ordinator.
4. Special needs co-ordinator.

Posts of Responsibility

Here are some actual examples.

A teacher with one additional point in the modern languages department at a large comprehensive school has a teaching load of 30 periods a week out of 35. In addition to teaching, she has the specific responsibility for a new language course being introduced into the Lower School. She is responsible for ordering materials, making sure that they are available when needed, and for liaison with the Media Resources Officer to see that equipment such as tape recorders, projectors etc are kept in working order and ready to use. She also has to initiate extra material for the course and arrange for work to be given to classes if any of the language teachers are away.

The head of a large science department with four points has much heavier responsibilities and consequently a lighter teaching load. She has under her four teachers with extra allowances and eight other full-time and part-time staff. She is also responsible for the work of the technicians in the laboratories. She has overall responsibility for all science courses offered in the school, including safety in the laboratories. She has to work closely with other departments, especially maths and remedial education. She is responsible for deciding how the department's budget should be spent and for helping and supporting any probationary teachers in the department.

As a contrast, here are the responsibilities of a deputy head of a small primary school, taken from a job description drawn up by the head.

> The person to be appointed will need to be an experienced teacher with a wide range of teaching experience and a versatile and modern approach to problems. Although the post will not involve the full-time responsibility for a class, the deputy head should be able to take over any class when necessary. The responsibilities will include a large part of the day-to-day administration of the school and general timetabling, arrangement of duties, stock control and co-ordination of stock ordering, overseeing attendance and welfare problems. The deputy will have overall responsibility for assessment and record keeping. Discipline in the school is the concern of all staff but the deputy head will have to mediate and act in a supportive role. The traits of insight, sympathy and understanding for others will help in maintaining cordial relationships. The ability to approach and form a positive liaison with parents of children, especially those children with problems, will ensure that the school's role is calm and supportive.

As you can see, there is a lot more to being a successful teacher than liking children and being good at a particular subject.

Induction and In-Service Training

When you leave college with your professional qualification, you cannot be regarded as a fully-fledged teacher. Even in England and Wales where the probationary period has now been abolished, 'First Appointments' or 'NQTs' (Newly Qualified Teachers) are still normally given special help.

In Scotland you still have to complete satisfactorily a probationary period of two years before registration by the General Teaching Council as a fully qualified teacher. In Northern Ireland the period is usually one year.

A survey of Her Majesty's Inspectors found that many new teachers were dissatisfied with their training and felt they needed a great deal of help in their early years of teaching. They criticised the lack of time on learning about how to control pupils and manage their classes. Primary teachers felt that they had not had enough preparation to teach all the subjects now required at primary schools. They all felt they were not taught enough about computers, special needs, and the administrative chores they had to do. The arrangements to help young teachers have improved since then. There will normally be one or more teachers in the school who act as tutors to the probationers on the staff. LEA advisers will offer help and support, and many LEAs arrange special courses and meetings for them. Group discussions and workshops with new teachers from other schools are very popular.

In the same way, far more attention is now given to in-service training for teachers, called INSET for short. This is to improve their teaching skills, to keep them up to date with new developments in their subject and to help them cope with the rapidly changing needs of the school population. Most LEAs will have a Professional Development Centre offering a variety of courses for teachers in and out of school hours. Higher education institutions also provide courses and seminars. It is estimated that more than half of serving teachers undertake some INSET every year.

Under Local Management of Schools, schools are now responsible for paying for INSET for their own staff. Courses are generally chosen to meet the priorities of the school development plan as well as the personal development of the teacher.

In order to reduce the amount of time that teachers are away from the classroom for training, new regulations allow schools to pay staff who volunteer to go to INSET out of school hours.

Here are some examples of what may be on offer:

Food Technology: making sense of the orders: one day

Primary Science: choice of one-day courses

The experience of mentoring in schools: one-day course

Primary School Development Planning in Action; one-day seminar

Diploma in Specific Learning Difficulties: 30 days over one academic year

Primary NQTs PE, Music and Art: six days over one term

Register for six years with a university and take a modular course in whatever subjects you choose, leading to an MEd.

The HEADLAMP scheme for helping new heads to acquire management skills.

Chapter 3

Finding a Job

Once you are qualified, how do you find a job? The best sources are the educational press, where most vacancies are advertised. These include *The Times Educational Supplement*, published weekly on Fridays and the Education Guardian published in the *Guardian* every Tuesday. Some LEAs have their own internal newsletter. If you want to teach in a particular area, write to the LEA and ask what chances there are of getting a job in your subject. Quite a few students get their first job through contacts made during their teaching practice.

Under the terms of the 1944 Education Act no teacher can be disqualified from a job or promotion because of religious beliefs (or lack of them) apart from certain special posts for teaching religious studies in voluntary schools. However, voluntary aided schools can specify religious belief as one of their selection criteria.

How to Apply

The arrangements for applying for a job vary widely from one LEA to another. In schools with delegated budgets (LMS 'local management of schools'), the governing body is responsible for recruitment and selection of staff, though much of this work will normally be delegated to the head. In some areas, all candidates for first appointments are interviewed by LEA officers at the Education Offices; in others the head will do the interviewing. In the case of posts of responsibility and above, the governing body of the school will usually be involved in shortlisting and interviewing candidates. Facing an appointments panel of governors can be disconcerting, but remember that lay governors can often be more sympathetic than the professionals. They know the school well and want the best candidate for *their* school. They may be more likely to make allowances for nerves and shyness.

Whatever the procedure, there are some important points you should bear in mind. Do read with care the application form and any accompanying information. Answer the questions on the form leaving no gaps or omissions. It always pays to follow the instructions on the form, even if you are having to apply for many jobs and have your own application and biographical notes already prepared. In most cases you will receive a job description and selection criteria for the post. Do try to make sure that you follow these when completing your application. The selection panel will want to know whether you meet their criteria. It makes it easier for the panel if all the applications are in the same format.

Most forms will have some space for you to give a personal statement of your reasons for applying for the job. Take care in preparing this to make it relevant, not too long, and easy to read. Pages of handwritten script are a minus for any applicant, however much you have to say.

Preparing for the Interview

Although interviews and interviewers vary – some are more skilful than others – it is helpful to know that more and more people use the job description and person specification to provide some structure and focus to the proceedings. A person specification describes the qualities needed to perform the functions listed in the job description, usually under four main headings:

- *Qualifications:* the education and training needed to do the job.
- *Experience:* teaching and non-teaching. Don't forget to draw attention to any experience outside teaching that may be relevant.
- *Knowledge:* required for that particular post.
- *Skills:* this may include personal skills such as teamwork, communicating with parents; proven ability in raising pupils' self-esteem.

If there are factors that would exclude anyone these should be stated in advance.

It is illegal for questions likely to be regarded as discriminatory to be put to candidates, so interviewees should not be asked questions bearing directly or indirectly on religious beliefs, sexual orientation, marital status, political affiliations, union membership or family responsibilities.

Do prepare yourself for the interview by finding out as much as possible in advance about the school. It is usual to ask candidates to visit the school before the interview, but if this is not done, ask the head if you can spend a morning or afternoon there. For example, if you are told that the school uses a particular maths course, and you have no experience of it, at least make the effort to find out something about it beforehand. Then you can talk intelligently about it while explaining that you have no personal experience of teaching it.

Try to have an answer ready if the panel asks the question, 'Would you accept the post if offered?' If you ask for time to consider, this may damage your chances of being offered the job when there is little to choose between you and the other candidates.

When you have been employed as a teacher for some time and are looking for promotion, the interviewers will be very interested to see what extra-curricular work you undertake in your present post, and what efforts you have made to improve your qualifications and to acquire new skills and knowledge through in-service training, as well as looking at your professional experience.

Conditions of Employment

There are now several different kinds of school in which education is provided free to pupils. *County schools* are built, staffed and fully provided for by the LEA; *voluntary schools* were established originally by churches and charities but their running costs are now paid by the LEA while they receive grants towards their building costs direct from central government; *city technology colleges* are funded by grants from the DFEE and donations from local industry; *grant-maintained schools* which have opted out of local authority control, and which are run entirely by the governors, receive grants from the DFEE.

Teachers in county schools are employed and paid by the LEA. In voluntary schools they are employed by the governors and paid by the LEA. In city technology colleges and grant-maintained schools, they are employed and paid by the governors. The pay and conditions of service remain very similar. The LEA can dismiss teachers in county schools, and has to sanction dismissal in voluntary schools. The governors can dismiss teachers in city technology colleges and grant-maintained schools. If a school has a delegated budget under Local Management of Schools, the governing body has the right to hire and fire teachers without reference to the LEA.

In the past it has been difficult to dismiss teachers, but now that schools are managing their own budgets, poor performance in the classroom is less tolerated. (Conversely, there are more opportunities to reward good performance.) Staffing takes up about 75–80 per cent of a school's costs so governing bodies are naturally keen to get good value for money. However, teachers are of course protected in the same way as other employees under employment protection legislation. Governing bodies on the whole aim to be good employers and the last thing they want is to end up in an industrial tribunal defending a charge of unfair dismissal.

One of the results of this new freedom and of the ending of probation is that teachers may at first be offered one-year contracts instead of a guaranteed long-term job. There is also a tendency to appoint heads on fixed-term contracts.

As well as full-time teaching, there are also appointments as part-time staff, temporary terminal staff (which means that you have security of tenure for a term at a time), and peripatetic teachers, who regularly visit a number of schools, eg for musical instrument lessons. In urban areas, there are often teacher supply agencies, who provide staff for schools on a temporary basis.

When you are appointed you will receive a copy of an agreement setting out the terms and conditions of your employment. These prescribe the minimum period of notice that you must give, the type of post, salary and other important information. Grant-maintained schools and city technology colleges have their own contracts of employment which may differ from the standard LEA contract. Teaching appointments are, of course, subject to all the general provisions about employment laid down in the Employment Protection Acts, the Sex and Race Discrimination Acts and redundancy payments legislation.

All teachers can participate in the teachers' superannuation scheme, run according to regulations laid down by the Secretary of State. The scheme is administered by the DFEE and has the advantage that when you change your job or move to another LEA there is no need to change your pension arrangements.

Teachers' Unions

There are a number of teachers' organisations, including unions for certain classes of teacher, such as heads, or teachers in further and higher education. Teachers in maintained schools have a choice of four: the National Union of Teachers (NUT), the National Association of Schoolmasters/Union of Women Teachers (NAS/UWT), the Association of Teachers and Lecturers (formerly AMMA), and the Professional Association of Teachers (PAT), one condition of whose membership is the renunciation of the right to strike. You will find a full list of teachers' organisations, together with advertisements from the various unions that may help you to decide which, if any, you want to join, in the *Education Yearbook*. The unions are very active in the defence of their members' interests; this can be particularly valuable to teachers threatened with legal action, for example in cases of alleged negligence, or in disciplinary hearings.

Other Openings for Qualified Teachers

In the educational world, there are many jobs outside the schools that are open to qualified teachers. For example, candidates for all the top jobs in educational administration in the LEAs, from Chief Education Officer downwards, preferably have some experience of teaching. Some LEAs continue to employ advisers and inspectors to support their schools, who often provide teams of inspectors for the new OFSTED inspection system. There are also independent companies tendering for OFSTED work and many education consultancy firms, filling the gap left by the reduction in the number of LEA advisers.

Educational broadcasting on radio and television is constantly expanding, particularly with local broadcasting and the possibility of cable. Educational research is another field. You could decide to go on to teach in higher, further or adult education, or training in industry. There are many opportunities for travel as a teacher of English as a second language. The prospects do not have to be limited to teaching in a school, although the majority of teachers find this the most satisfying way of using their training.

Part 2:
How to Qualify as a Teacher

Introduction

There are a number of different ways of qualifying as a teacher, and which one you choose depends on your personal preferences, taking into account your academic qualifications. It is a good idea to talk this over with your school or college careers teacher or the local education authority careers adviser if you can, as they should be able to give you advice based on their knowledge both of the colleges and courses, and of yourself.

Every local education authority has access to a careers service, which is open to all those who are receiving any kind of education, whether full time or part time. The careers advisers should have up-to-date information about all kinds of courses, and are able to help you to apply for places and grants, so do not hesitate to make use of their free services. You can get the address from the Education Offices, or they are listed in the *Education Yearbook*, which should be in your local reference library.

When you have made up your mind that you want to be a teacher, you need to take two important decisions, usually at a fairly early stage:

(a) which age group you want to teach; and
(b) what subject you want to specialise in.

On the whole, if you want to teach in secondary, further or higher education, it is probably better to take a subject degree course, either combined with or followed by professional training. Most primary school teachers train through BEd courses at colleges of education or universities, although some take a degree followed by postgraduate training. The National Curriculum's demands on primary school teachers mean that primary schools need more specialists than in the past.

Chapter 4

Teaching Qualifications

If you want to teach in a state school, you must have recognised qualifications. In England and Wales these are decided by the Department for Education and Employment, in Scotland by the General Teaching Council, and in Northern Ireland by the Department of Education.

England and Wales

For teachers entering the profession at the present time there are five acceptable qualifications:

1. A BEd degree: you can take a four-year course for an honours Bachelor of Education degree or a two-year shortened BEd.
2. A first degree (ordinary or honours) in any subject, normally a three-year course, followed by a year's professional training for the Postgraduate Certificate of Education (PGCE).
3. For a few specified subjects, there are two-year training courses leading to a certificate giving qualified teacher status.
4. A degree other than BEd which is obtained through a four-year course that includes a teaching qualification.
5. A two-year on-the-job training scheme based at a school giving 'Licensed Teacher' status to those fulfilling the following criteria:
   (a) UK citizens who should be at least 24, have GCSEs (grades A–C) or their equivalent in English and maths, or have successfully completed two years of full-time higher education.

(b) (i) Overseas entrants who should have an overseas
teaching qualification of comparable status to those
recognised under the EC Directive, namely recognition
as a qualified teacher after three years of higher education and training.

(ii) Overseas entrants who have British or overseas
degrees recognised under the former Burnham Committee.

You can obtain the first four qualifications in the following ways:

☐ University BEd degree course
☐ University combined degree course incorporating a teaching
qualification
☐ University degree course followed by PGCE taken at univer-
sity or college of higher education
☐ Degree plus school-centred initial teacher training (SCITT)
☐ Degree plus two-year PGCE conversion course to teach short-
age subjects
☐ Colleges and institutions of higher education BEd course
☐ Colleges and institutions of higher education degree course
followed by PGCE
☐ Two-year Diploma of Higher Education (DipHE) course, then
transfer to the third year of a degree course for BEd
☐ Two-year DipHE course, then transfer to the third year of a
degree course followed by PGCE
☐ Qualifications and experience in business studies, craft design
and technology, music, physics, chemistry, maths or modern
languages, followed by a one- or two-year specialist training
course, or shorter BEd course
☐ Degree plus Open University distance learning PGCE course.

BEd Courses
BEd courses combine the study of educational theory and practice, child development, psychology, and sociology with detailed
study of your chosen specialist subjects. Teaching practice in
schools is an important element of the course.

University Degree Courses
With the reorganisation of higher education, former polytechnics
now have university status and award their own degrees. The
quality of these degrees is monitored by the Higher Educational

Funding Council. Any colleges of higher education or specialist colleges which do not have university status or are not attached to a university have their degrees validated by one of the university institutions.

University degrees may be single-subject or combined-subject. The former polytechnics are more likely to offer wider courses and project-based courses than the traditional universities. They may rely more on continuous assessment than annual exams to test students' competence. Some institutions offer modular courses where you can choose your own programmes of studies from a wide range on offer.

In Scotland the pattern is for four-year courses which Scottish students usually begin at age 17 after taking the Scottish Higher Certificate. They tend to be more broadly based than English degree courses. The first year is at a similar level to the second year of a GCE A-level course.

DipHE Courses

The DipHE is intended to be both a qualification in its own right and an alternative route towards a degree. It is very useful if you are uncertain about whether or not you want to go into teaching, as it allows you to continue your education for another two years before you have to decide. Courses have to be validated by a university, and may be single-subject or multi-disciplinary. Some colleges run a common course for the DipHE and degree students, so that you do not have to decide straight away which course to follow.

Postgraduate Certificate of Education Courses (PGCE)

These are run at universities and colleges, and aim to give you the professional skills you need to be a successful teacher, as well as some study of the theory of child development and education. They include at least 24 weeks' teaching practice in schools.

Two-Year Teacher Education Courses

These are intended to supply professional teaching skills to people with special qualifications that have no teaching content. They include courses for people who want to teach craft or commercial subjects and training for people who want to qualify in teaching a musical instrument.

Entrance Requirements

The same basic requirements apply to all these courses, though you may be exempted from some of them if you want to teach a practical subject.

Age

Most colleges expect you to be 18 by 31 December in the year in which you begin the course, but some will accept younger people – the prospectus will tell you. There is no maximum age.

Academic Qualifications

Anyone taking any teaching qualifications must have GCSE (Grade C or above) or its equivalent in English language and maths. All applicants must be able to communicate clearly in spoken and written English. From September 1998 all applicants for primary training must have GCSE in a science subject. General National Vocational Qualifications (GNVQs) and National Vocational Qualifications (NVQs) at an appropriate level may be acceptable, depending on the content of the course. Some colleges offer a special exam to mature students without GCSEs. The following are acceptable:

English Language

- GCSE (Grade C or above) in English language
- Use of English
- GCE A level in English literature – these being offered by any Board
- *Associated Examining Board* GCSE (Grade C or above) in English language (professional and business use)
- *Joint Matriculation Board* GCSE (Grade C or above) in additional English
- GCE A level in general studies
- University Entrance Test in English
- University Entrance Test in English (overseas).

Mathematics

- GCSE (Grade C or above) in mathematics
- GCE A level in mathematics or in any subject with mathematics in its title
- GCE A level in statistics
- GCSE (Grade C or above) in additional mathematics – these

being offered by any Board

☐ *Associated Examining Board* GCSE (Grade C or above) in commercial mathematics
☐ General mathematics
☐ Modern mathematics
☐ Technical mathematics
☐ Technical (building) mathematics
☐ *University of London* GCSE (Grade C or above) in applied mathematics
☐ Mathematics and theoretical mechanics
☐ Pure mathematics
☐ *Oxford and Cambridge Schools Examination Board* GCSE (Grade C or above) in general mathematics
☐ *Joint Matriculation Board* GCSE (Grade C or above) in commercial mathematics
☐ GCSE (Grade C or above) in mathematical studies
☐ SUB commercial mathematics and statistics.

Colleges may accept other examinations as an alternative and you should check with them before applying. You then have to be able to satisfy the entrance requirements of the college to which you are applying. These are usually based on GCSE and A levels according to the following formulae:

Five passes at GCSE (Grade C or above) – at least two at A level
Four passes at GCSE (Grade C or above) – three at A level
A good pass at ONC, OND or the equivalent BTEC, GNVQ, NVQ, qualifications are also acceptable to many colleges.

Some colleges will accept candidates for practical subjects with only one A level, as long as their standard of work in the practical subject is very high. Many degree courses will require a higher standard than a Grade E pass at A level. To get a place on a popular course at any college you will probably need better grades and a wider range of subjects.

You must check very carefully with the requirements listed in the prospectus of the college before applying for a course. Far too many people apply for courses for which they are not qualified.

Protection of Children
Local education authorities are required to check with police 'the

possible criminal background of those who apply to work with children'. Before applying for teacher training you need to take advice if you have any criminal convictions. (See DFEE circular 9/93, Protection of Children: Disclosure of criminal background of those with access to children.)

Scotland

Courses of initial teacher training are offered by six institutions: Moray House Institute, Northern College, St Andrew's College and the Universities of Paisley, Stirling and Strathclyde. You can get full details about qualifications from the Advisory Service on Entry to Teaching in Scotland, run by the General Teaching Council for Scotland, 5 Royal Terrace, Edinburgh EH7 5AF; 0131 556 0072.

You may not teach in a maintained or grant-aided school in Scotland unless you are registered with the General Teaching Council. If you obtain a qualification from a Scottish college of education you are automatically entitled to register. The Council welcomes applications for registration from teachers who have qualified in another part of the United Kingdom or abroad.

There are separate Scottish qualifications for primary education and for secondary education.

Teaching Qualifications (Primary Education)
These qualify you to teach general subjects in a primary school or department. You can obtain the qualifications in the following ways.

    (a) A four-year course leading to a BEd (Hons) degree.
    (b) A degree from a UK university (including the Open University) followed by a one-year PGCE course.

Teaching Qualifications (Secondary Education)
These qualify you to teach a particular subject or subjects in secondary schools. You can obtain the qualifications in the following ways.

    (a) A university degree course (including the Open University) followed by a one-year PGCE course.
    (b) A BEd (Hons) in Technological Education (four-year course)
    (c) A BEd (Hons) in Music (four-year course)

(d) A BEd (Hons) in Physical Education (four-year course)

(e) Concurrent degree in a limited number of subjects.

Entry Requirements

The following are the *minimum* entry requirements only. Provided these are met the teacher education institutions then decide on whether or not to accept a particular applicant. They may look for additional qualifications and for evidence that applicants have the necessary qualities for and commitment to teaching as a career.

The minimum entry requirements for admission to training as a primary teacher are:

(a) For a four-year BEd course:
- SCE Higher Grade passes in at least three subjects (one of which must be English); and
- SCE Standard Grade awards in two other subjects.
- Mathematics must be included as one of the passes or awards.

Note

Admission to a four-year BEd course from academic session 2000/2001 will require an award in mathematics at a minimum of Standard Grade Credit Level (Grades 1 or 2)

(b) For a one-year PGCE course:
- degree from a UK higher education institution or degree of an equivalent standard from an institution outwith the UK;
- SCE Higher Grade pass in English; and
- SCE Standard Grade award in mathematics.

Note

Admission to the one-year PGCE course from academic session 2000/2001 will require an award in mathematics at a minimum of Standard Grade Credit Level (Grades 1 or 2).

Teacher education institutions (TEIs) should satisfy themselves that the contents of an applicant's previous education, including the degree, provides the necessary foundation for work as a primary teacher. They will therefore normally be looking for evidence of prior learning in at least two of the following areas (in addition to English and mathematics): science; social studies; expressive arts; religious and moral education; technology; modern foreign languages.

All enquiries about the acceptability of non-UK degrees should, in the first instance, be directed to TEIs. When necessary, TEIs will seek the advice of the GTC.

The Teaching Qualification (Secondary Education)

General Points
The Teaching Qualification (Secondary Education) is awarded in a particular subject or subjects of the secondary school curriculum after successful completion of one of the following courses:

(a) 4-year course leading to a BEd degree in music, physical education (PE) or technological education;

(b) combined degree (sometimes known as concurrent degree) including subject study, study of education and school experience; or

(c) one-year Postgraduate Certificate of Education (PGCE) course following upon a degree.

Teaching Qualifications (Secondary Education) can be awarded in the following subjects:

Agriculture & Horticulture	English	Modern Foreign Languages
Art and Design	Gaelic	Modern Studies
Biology	Geography	Music
Business Studies	Geology	Nautical Studies
Chemistry	Greek	Physical Education
Classics	History	Physics
Community Languages	Economic History	Religious Education
Computing	Home Economics	Science
Drama	Latin	Technological Education
Economics	Mathematics	

It is possible to gain a teaching qualification in more than one subject. Not all subjects may be available in a particular session with some only available at certain TEIs. Some subjects may be available only in conjunction with other subjects.

For some courses such as PE and music, applicants will need to demonstrate competence in practical skills. This may require them to undergo practical tests set by the TEI.

All enquiries about availability of courses should be directed to TEIs.

Northern Ireland

To teach in Northern Ireland you must have a qualification recognised by the Northern Ireland Department of Education. Broadly speaking, the qualifications it recognises are similar to those laid down by the Department of Education for teachers in England and Wales following the standard routes to qualified teacher status. Full details may be obtained from the Northern Ireland Department of Education, Teachers Branch, Waterside House, 75 Duke Street, Londonderry BT47 1FP; 01504 319000.

Chapter 5

Where to Study

Choosing a Course

Having decided what route you want to follow, you next have to choose a college and a course. There is perhaps more variety in the content of education studies than in many other subjects, and it is very important to find out the content and structure of courses before you decide. Secondary phase courses now have to include much longer periods in school on teaching practice than formerly – at least 24 weeks in a PGCE course, or 32 weeks in a BEd course. Similar regulations may be proposed for primary phase courses.

You should first consult *The NATFHE Handbook of Initial Teacher Training*, which is published annually by the National Association of Teachers in Further and Higher Education, Linneys ESL, Newgate Lane, Mansfield NG18 2PA. This should be in your careers library or local reference library. It gives details of all the teacher-training courses available and describes them briefly.

Then you need to look carefully at college prospectuses. You may be able to narrow down your choice by looking quickly through a large number of prospectuses at your local library or school careers library, but having done this it is best to send off to your shortlist of colleges for your own copy of their prospectus. All you have to do is send a request to the college, addressed to the Registrar or the Admissions Officer (example overleaf). As they have many enquiries it helps if you enclose a self-addressed and stamped gummed label (not envelope).

In the case of the universities of Cambridge, London, Oxford and Wales, write to the individual college, not the university.

Specimen of prospectus enquiry

College prospectus enquiry
Please send me information about entrance requirements, courses, fees, residence etc.
(word this as appropriate)

BLOCK   Name ....
CAPITALS
PLEASE   Address ....

               ....

Proposed course(s) ....

.... Proposed year of entry ....

Signed .... Date ....

Choosing a College

Choosing a course and a college necessarily tend to go together, but it is particularly important to find out about the college as well as the academic content of the course. Many colleges offering education courses are often fairly small institutions. Even when they are part of a university, they may be isolated from the mainstream of student life. This has advantages and disadvantages and suits some people better than others, and only you can make up your mind what kind of institution you would prefer.

As well as reading the official prospectus it is worth having a look at any alternative student prospectuses that may be available. You may need to take the alternative prospectuses with a pinch of salt, but they do give a new perspective to the official information.

Talking to students on the course you are interested in can be very enlightening. You may have an opportunity to do this if you visit some of the colleges before making up your mind which to apply to. Most colleges are very happy to welcome visitors, either to formally arranged Open Days or privately arranged visits. Many arrange special courses and conferences for sixth-form students.

If you are unable to travel long distances to visit colleges it would be quite useful to visit the nearest one to your home, just to see what a college of education is like.

Mature Students

Almost all colleges give special consideration to the problems of candidates over 25 who may not have the academic qualifications required from school leavers. The best way to find out what your chances are is to write direct to the institution which is your first choice and find out from there what its policy is before making a formal application.

If it is a long time since you have any experience of studying you may be asked to take some kind of refresher course or to improve your basic qualifications before taking on teacher training. This is particularly likely if you do not have the minimum English language and maths passes. The Teacher Training Agency (TTA) publish a helpful leaflet Access to Higher Education, which gives details of access courses, usually provided in colleges of further education, which can help you to qualify. Colleges are anxious to recruit more teachers from ethnic minorities, who are under-represented in the profession.

If you are restricted in your choice of colleges and subsequently jobs because of family commitments, the DFEE recommends that you discuss local employment prospects with your LEA before applying for a course. It is clearly a good idea to choose one of the subjects in which there is a shortage of teachers if you can.

Licensed Teachers Scheme

Education authorities (LEAs) decide whether or not to employ people as licensed teachers. Apply direct to them.

Students with Disabilities

Many teachers with disabilities have pursued successful careers and there are many reasons why more students with disabilities should be encouraged to pursue a teaching career. As well as their own personal contribution to a post, teachers with disabilities can provide an important and positive role model for children with special educational needs in both mainstream and special schools.

DFEE Medical Regulations

Students with a disability will have to satisfy the college to which they apply that they can cope with the course and with teaching afterwards. Details of DFEE requirements on the health of teachers are explained in DFE Circular No 13/93, Physical and Mental Fitness to Teach of Teachers and Entrants to Initial Teacher Training. The Circular points out that 'In considering the medical, physical and mental fitness of people for training as teachers the principal concern of examining medical advisers must be the health, education and welfare of pupils or students likely to be in their care.' It gives advice on whether various diseases should be a bar to teaching, for example it states that HIV infection should not in itself be a reason for refusal of an applicant. If you are at all concerned about your fitness to teach, discuss this with a specialist medical or careers adviser, but do not be put off without first investigating all the possibilities fully.

Applying

Most colleges have an adviser or co-ordinator for students with disabilities, so it is advisable to contact them, to discuss how they may be able to help with any special needs you have, before making your application for a teaching course. If the college is fully acquainted with your needs, it will be in a better position to help you.

Sources of Help and Advice

Skill: National Bureau for Students with Disabilities is a voluntary organisation, involved in developing opportunities for people with physical or sensory disabilities or learning difficulties in all aspects of post-16 education, training and employment. Skill runs an information and advice service for any member of the public with an enquiry about study, training or work. The Information Officer can be contacted at 336 Brixton Road, London SW9 7AA; or on 0171 978 9890 Mon-Fri, 1.30-4.30, and can help with enquiries on matters such as funding, benefits, applying to college etc. A number of useful publications and free information sheets are available, including *A Guide to Higher Education for People with Disabilities – Part 1: Making Your Application* and *Part 2: Guide to Access and Facilities*.

RADAR (the Royal Association for Disability and Rehabilitation), 12 City Forum, 250 City Road, London EC1V 8AF; 0171 250 3222; can help with queries on teaching and disability, and has access to a wide range of information sources.

Specialist Subjects: Art and Design, Drama

If you want to teach any of these subjects you can either take a BEd in the usual way, specialising in that field, or you can study for a degree course or equivalent in the subject and then do a Postgraduate Certificate in Education.

Art and Design
For courses leading to the PGCE in Art or Design you have to apply through the Clearing House for Postgraduate Courses in Art and Design Education, Penn House, 9 Broad Street, Hereford HR4 9EP; 01432 266 653.

Colleges Offering These Courses
Bretton Hall College of Further Education, Wakefield
Brighton University
Cardiff Institute of Higher Education
University of Central England, Birmingham
De Montfort University, Leicester
John Moores University, Liverpool
London:
    Goldsmiths' College, University of London
    Institute of Education, University of London
Manchester Metropolitan University
Middlesex University
Reading University
University of Ulster
Westminster College, Oxford

Drama
Drama is offered as a main subject in a number of BEd courses, and is also an option in Combined Studies courses for a BA degree. There are also BA degree courses in Performing Arts or Theatre Arts, and a few single-subject drama degree courses. The practical content in all these courses varies widely from one to another, so

you should check carefully beforehand what the syllabus includes and whether it is what you want.

People who are considering the possibility of becoming a drama teacher but who do not want to take a BEd need to check carefully that the course they propose to take will be accepted as a suitable basis for taking a PGCE to qualify as a drama teacher.

Degree courses with a drama component are listed in the UCAS booklet.

Teaching Children with Special Needs

All children, however severe their disabilities, have the right to an education that develops their faculties to the fullest possible extent. In the past, it has been general for children regarded as handicapped to be segregated in special schools and units, but since the passage of the 1981 Education Act there have been many changes in the way children with special needs are educated. The tendency is for more and more of these children to be educated along with their contemporaries in mainstream schools, with individual support where necessary from teachers and assistants. This move towards integration has been helped by the fact that it is now recognised that many more children than those in special schools will need some kind of special help during their school career.

Integration will mean that many more teachers will need to have some knowledge and understanding of children with disabilities, and the skills needed to help them. Special education is provided in a great variety of schools and units. There are day and boarding schools for children with specific handicaps such as blindness and deafness, units attached to ordinary schools, and hospital schools. There are also arrangements for individual teaching for children who are unable to attend a school at all.

The DFEE regulations prescribe special qualifications for teaching children with some disabilities. You can obtain these by taking a special course after you have qualified. Teachers in special schools are expected to have had some experience of teaching in mainstream schools.

Special Qualifications

Teaching Children with Visual Impairment
You may not teach blind children unless you have a qualification
approved by the Secretary of State, except that you can teach
them while studying for one of these qualifications. The Royal
National Institute for the Blind (RNIB) publishes a free leaflet
'Working with Visually Impaired Children' with details of approved courses. It is obtainable free from RNIB Education Information Services, 226 Great Portland Street, London W1N 6AA;
0171 388 1266.

Teaching Deaf or Partially Hearing Children
You may not teach deaf children unless you have a qualification
approved by the Secretary of State, except that you can teach
them while studying for one of these qualifications. The Royal
National Institute for Deaf People (RNID), in collaboration with
the British Association for Teachers of the Deaf, publishes a free
leaflet, updated annually, about approved qualifications. Obtainable free from RNID, 105 Gower Street, London WC1E 6AH;
0171 387 6033.

Teaching Children Who Are Both Blind And Deaf
You should have one of the qualifications for teaching deaf
children, or one of those for teaching blind children.

*Teaching Children In Special Units For Partially Hearing Chil-
dren Attached To Ordinary Schools*
You should have one of the qualifications for teaching deaf
children *before* beginning work in the unit.

Extra allowances may be paid to teachers with these qualifications.

Teaching Children with Learning Difficulties
Special schools for children with learning difficulties are usually
of two kinds: those for children with moderate learning difficulties (MLD schools) and those for children with severe learning
difficulties (SLD schools). The DFEE does not prescribe any
additional qualification for teaching children with learning difficulties, but there are special options in BEd and PGCE courses

at many colleges, as well as special postgraduate diplomas and masters' degrees. Details are available in the *Handbook of Degree and Advanced Courses*, see p 91.

In-Service Training

Schools may offer training courses for teachers in special education or arrange secondment to college courses. The encouragement is very practical, consisting of time off and payment of fees etc.

Scotland

The first school in Britain for the education of deaf children was opened in Edinburgh in 1769 and Moray House remains an important centre for the education of teachers of those with hearing impairment. Registered teachers can take a series of courses to assist them in teaching children with specific educational needs.

Northern Ireland

Teachers in special schools must be qualified to teach in primary or secondary schools. The Department of Education insists on special qualifications for teachers of blind and deaf children.

Chapter 6

How to Apply

The arrangements for making applications to courses of education have been simplified over recent years. There are some differences between England and Wales, Scotland and Northern Ireland, which are explained in each section.

University Degree Courses

All applications for first degree courses at universities and their affiliated colleges throughout the United Kingdom have to go through UCAS – the Universities and Colleges Admissions Service. The only exception is the Open University to which you apply direct. Full details about how to apply for any university first degree course, including the complex arrangements for Oxford and Cambridge, are set out in the *UCAS Handbook*, obtainable free from your school or college or, if you are not currently a student, direct from UCAS, Fulton House, Jessop Avenue, Cheltenham, GL50 3SH; 01242 227788.

Briefly, you choose your universities and list them in institution code number order on your application form. You also give details of your academic qualifications. Most universities will lay down general 'matriculation' requirements for all students regardless of the course, so make sure that your qualifications satisfy these as well as the ones required by the course. There have been cases where a student accepted by a department has been rejected by the university on these grounds.

There are two other important parts of the form: a space for you to describe your interests and activities, and a space for your school or college to write a confidential report on you. With so many well-qualified candidates, these two personal descriptions are often very important in helping university admissions tutors to select candidates.

It is a good idea to apply as early as you can, particularly for places on a popular teacher education course. Include as much evidence as you can about your interests and abilities concerned with teaching and working with children.

You return the forms to UCAS complete with your application fee. They are scanned and reduced in size and then sent simultaneously to each of your chosen universities or colleges which decide whether or not to interview you, or whether or not to offer you a place without interview. An offer may be either conditional, ie dependent on your obtaining certain grades in your forthcoming examinations (A levels, Scottish Highers, etc), or unconditional. You do not have to reply to any offers until you are notified of all university decisions. Important dates are:

1 September	Opening date for applications
15 October	Closing date for applications including Oxford and Cambridge
15 December	Closing date for all other applications.

In August and September, after the examination results are out, clearing takes place. People who have no offers at that stage, or who have failed to achieve the required grades for their conditional offers, are given another chance to apply for vacancies – UCAS estimate that about 8.2 per cent of places are finally allocated at this stage, so it is not a forlorn hope.

Teacher Education Courses at Colleges and Institutions of Higher Education, Universities and Colleges of Education

England and Wales

Courses for the education of teachers are all now contained within the UCAS scheme (see above). Applicants must check carefully with the college they wish to apply to and follow the relevant application instructions.

Courses included are:

(a) BA/BSc four-year course with initial teacher training.
(b) Four-year BEd (Hons) degree.
(c) Shortened two-year BEd course.

(d) Two-year Diploma of Higher Education course which, in most cases, can lead to a BEd or other degree. *Note.* At some institutions there is a common first (or two) year(s) which permits deferment of choice of future qualification.
(e) Three-year BA (Hons) course at Laban Centre for Movement and Dance.
(f) Two-year specialist course in a few subjects.

What Offers Do Colleges Usually Make?
You can find out from *Complete Degree Course Offers* by Brian Heap, published annually by Trotman Publishing, what the average requirement for degree courses is and the competition for places at the colleges and universities offering first degrees. The minimum requirement for a BEd course is two Es, but popular courses are likely to make higher offers. For example, you would need BBC or BCC for many courses at the longer-established universities.

You might be accepted with one A Level for a course requiring special artistic or craft ability. Remember, however, that the selection processes take account of many other attributes besides academic success, and performance at interview is a determining factor.

Scotland
Anyone wishing to take a subject degree or four-year BEd course or concurrent degree should apply to UCAS in the normal way. Individual institutions will supply full details about the courses they offer – including the subjects to be studied and the arrangements for school experience placements, entry qualifications and selection procedures.

The number of students admitted to teacher training courses is limited and it is possible that a college may decide not to mount a particular course depending on overall intake quotas. It is also possible that no vacancies will be available at the second and third choice colleges for students who are unable to obtain a place at their first choice college.

Northern Ireland
If you wish to train as a teacher in Northern Ireland you have to write to the college of your choice there for a prospectus and application form. University applications are dealt with by UCAS in the usual way.

Postgraduate Certificate of Education (PGCE) Courses

England and Wales

All applications have to be made through the Graduate Teacher Training Registry (GTTR), Fulton House, Jessop Avenue, Cheltenham, Gloucestershire GL50 3SH; 01242 225868.

Full information about the courses is given in *The NATFHE Handbook of Initial Teacher Training* (see p 91), and a chart giving names and addresses of colleges and showing course content is included in the booklet issued by the GTTR with their application form.

Students wishing to join a school-centred course (SCITT) apply through the GTTR.

Entrance Qualifications

You should have, or be about to obtain, a degree awarded by a university or the CNAA. If you have an alternative qualification you should check with the GTTR and the college whether it is acceptable. You must also have GCSE maths and English (A-C), or the equivalent and, for primary teaching, science from 1998.

Application Procedure

Stage One. Write to GTTR for an application form and information and enclose a stamped, addressed envelope (10 x 7in). Forms are available from the beginning of September.

Stage Two. Complete the form, listing up to four choices of college. Give the names of two people: a principal reference who should be your college head or tutor or lecturer, who is prepared to write a reference for you, and a second referee who can give evidence about your character.

Stage Three. Any time after early September return the completed form with a fee of £6 by crossed postal order (not cheque) payable to Graduate Teacher Training Registry. The form must be sent to the GTTR, not your first choice college. If you have to delay returning the form, ask the GTTR for its latest vacancy list, so that you can avoid wasting a choice on a college that is already full.

Some colleges also issue their own application forms. If one of them is your first choice you should send the completed form to the college and not to the GTTR.

Stage Four. The GTTR will send your form to your first choice college. The college will inform you if it wants to interview you. You will not be offered a place without an interview. If it does not accept you, the GTTR will notify you and pass the form on to the next college on your list if suitable vacancies remain.

If none of your choices accepts you, the GTTR will continue passing on your form to colleges which still have suitable places, if you have indicated on your application form that this is acceptable.

Scotland
Applications for the one-year Postgraduate Certificate in Education (PGCE) should be made to TEACH, Teacher Education Admissions Clearing House, PO Box 165, Holyrood Road, Edinburgh EH8 8AT. Applications should be submitted as soon as possible after 1 October in the year before entry and the closing date is 15 December. For some of the secondary courses later applications are accepted, depending on the demand for the particular subject. Secondary school teachers qualify in a specific subject or subjects and so the institutions must be satisfied that the content and scope of the first degree course is acceptable. The terms are laid down in the memorandum on Entry Requirements which is issued by the Scottish Office Education Department and revised annually.

Northern Ireland
Colleges in Northern Ireland do not participate in the Graduate Training Registry Scheme. You have to apply direct to the college. Information about PGCE courses in Northern Ireland can be obtained from the Department of Education for Northern Ireland, Rathgael House, Balloo Road, Bangor, Co Down BT19 2PR.

Interviews

Do not be frightened by the prospect of an interview. All candidates will be interviewed for a BEd course, as personal attributes which may not come over in a written report can be of the greatest importance if an individual wants to teach. It is a good idea to get someone at your school or college to give you a mock interview, so that you can practise interviewing techniques and be warned against some of the more obvious faults. Remember that an interview is an opportunity for you to find out more about the course and the college, as well as for the college to get to know you. Take any chance of looking round the buildings and halls of residence and try to meet students, even if this is not specifically arranged for you. It may be worth writing to the students' union in advance to ask for their help.

It is best to play safe and dress conventionally, even though clothes are less formal nowadays, but don't wear your school uniform – that's going too far. Think beforehand about your answers to stock questions such as, '*Why do you want to come here?*', '*Why do you want to teach?*', but don't learn answers parrot-fashion and drag them in regardless of the question. Don't pretend you know the answer; try to respond positively. The most unrewarding candidate to interview is the one who seems impervious to the interviewer's probings. You must give the interviewer, as well as yourself, a chance.

Student Grants

As soon as you know that you have been offered a place on a course, you should contact the awards section of your local education authority in the first instance.

Full details about social security benefits and other issues can be obtained from the colleges or from the Student Financial Support Department, National Union of Students, 461 Holloway Road, London N7 6LJ; 0171 272 8900.

Grants for DipHE Students

The DipHE is a designated course, ie a course for which LEAs must pay a student grant. If you decide to transfer to a BEd course, the LEA must pay a grant covering the full course, a total of three years for an ordinary degree or four years for some honours degrees. Problems sometimes occur if the total length of time you are studying is more than three (or four) years. LEAs do not have to pay grants for the extra time, though many of them choose to do so. At a time when LEAs are having to make cuts in educational expenditure it may be more difficult to get 'topping-up' grants. So you may have to support yourself for one year of the course if you are taking more than the normal period to complete it.

How to Apply for Grants

It is a good idea to put in a preliminary application for a grant as soon as you make up your mind that you will be going on to some kind of higher education. You can then get all the necessary forms and evidence of parents' income etc ready in advance, even if you have not yet received a firm offer of a place. You should write to the LEA at the local Education Offices to ask for details and application forms, or they may be available at your school or college. Do not leave the grant application until the last minute, as the offices are very busy at the end of the summer and your application may be delayed. This means that you could be faced with large bills to pay at the beginning of term, and no grant to pay them with.

Because the amount of grant you receive depends on your parents' income, it is essential to have their co-operation in preparing the application form. Some students have had difficulties either because their parents refused to give details of their income or because they were unwilling, or unable, to pay the parental contribution towards the costs of studying at college, which the national scales of payment expect. LEAs will pay a minimum grant (fees only) to students whose parents have not completed the income statement on the application form, but this does not cover any living expenses so you would need some other source of income. If you do run into this kind of difficulty, your school or college tutor may be able to help by discussing the problem with your parents. Unfortunately, there is no scheme to help students whose parents do not support them, apart from the student loan scheme (see below), unless you have been self-supporting for at least three years before going to college.

Some colleges will accept private students, who are not eligible for any kind of grant. You should make it clear on your application form if you are in this category, and should be able to provide evidence that you have the resources needed.

Student Loans
The student loan scheme allows students to borrow from the Students Loan Company once they have begun their course. You must have a residence qualification and may not take out more than one loan during each year of the course. The loan does not have to be paid back until after you have finished the course. Full details and the necessary forms will be available from the college. A full explanation is also given in *Student Grants and Loans: A Brief Guide* published annually by the Department for Education.

Scotland
In Scotland grants are administered by the Scottish Office Education Department. You can get information about grants, loans, awards and allowances from the Student Awards Agency for Scotland, 3 Redheughs Rigg, South Gyle, Edinburgh EH12 9HH.

Northern Ireland
Details of grant procedures can be obtained from the Scholarships Branch, Department of Education for Northern Ireland, Rathgael House, Balloo Road, Bangor, Co Down BT19 2PR.

Chapter 7

Training Courses

Colleges Offering Initial Teacher Training

The colleges in the following list offer first degree courses and some also offer DipHE courses which can lead on to a degree course. Applications must be made through UCAS.

Key to type of course
  nlp=nursery/lower primary (3/4–8)
  lpr=lower primary (5–8)
  fst=first years of schooling (5–9)
  pr=primary (5–12)
  prm=primary/middle (5–13)
  upr=upper primary (7–12)
  upm=upper primary/middle (7–13)
  m=middle years of schooling (8/9–13)
  sec= secondary (11 upwards)

Name and address of institution	Type of course
Bangor, Normal College Bangor, Gwynedd LL57 2PX 01248 370171	nlp/upr
Bath College of Higher Education Newton Park, Bath BA2 9BN 01225 873701	lpr/upr/sec
Bedford College of Higher Education 37 Lansdowne Road, Bedford MK40 2BZ 01234 51966	pr/sec

Name and address of institution	Type of course
Birmingham, University of Central England Faculty of Education and Teacher Training Westbourne Road, Edgbaston Birmingham B15 3TN 0121 331 6101/6100	lpr/upr
Bognor Regis/Chichester West Sussex Institute of Higher Education The Dome, Upper Bognor Road Bognor Regis, West Sussex PO21 1HR 01243 865581	lpr/upr/sec
Bradford and Ilkley Community College Great Horton Road, Bradford BD7 1AY 01274 753026	lpr/upr/sec
Brentwood, Anglia Polytechnic University Sawyers Hall Lane, Brentwood Essex CM15 9BT 01277 216971	fst/upr/sec
Brighton University Falmer, Brighton, East Sussex BN1 9PH 01273 606622	nlp/upr/sec
Bristol, University of the West of England at Bristol Department of Education Redland Hill, Bristol BS6 6UZ 0117 974 1251	pr/sec
Canterbury, Christ Church College North Holmes Road, Canterbury Kent CT1 1QU 01227 762444	nlp/lpr/upr
Cardiff Institute of Higher Education Cyncoed, Cardiff CF2 6XD 01222 551111	pr
Welsh College of Music and Drama Castle Grounds, Cathays Park Cardiff CF1 3ER 01222 342854	sec
Carmarthen, Trinity College (CinW) Carmarthen, Dyfed, South Wales SA31 3EP 01267 237971	nlp/lpr/upm

Name and address of institution	Type of course
Cheltenham and Gloucester College of Higher Education The Park, Cheltenham Gloucestershire GL50 2RH 01242 513836	lpr/upr/sec
Crewe and Alsager College of Higher Education Crewe, Cheshire CW1 1DU 01270 500661	lpr/pr/upr/sec
Derby, Derbyshire College of Higher Education Mickleover, Derby DE3 5GX 01332 47181	nlp/upr
Exmouth, University of Plymouth Rolle Faculty of Education Exmouth, Devon EX8 2AT 01395 265344	nlp/upr
Hatfield, University of Hertfordshire Wall Hall, Aldenham, Watford WD2 8AT 01707 52511	lpr/upr
Huddersfield, University of Huddersfield Holly Bank Road, Lindley Huddersfield HD3 3BP 01484 25611	sec
Leeds Metropolitan University Beckett Park, Leeds LS6 3QS 0113 275 9061	nlp/upr/sec
Liverpool, John Moores University Craft Design and Technology Unit St Nicholas Centre Great Orford Street, Liverpool L3 5YD 0151 207 3581	sec
F L Calder Campus Dowsefield Lane Liverpool L18 3JJ 0151 428 4041	sec
I M Marsh Campus Barkhill Road, Liverpool L17 6BD 0151 724 2321	upr/sec

Name and address of institution	Type of course
London, Central School of Speech and Drama Embassy Theatre, Eton Avenue London NW3 3HY 0171 722 8183	sec
Kingston University Kingston Hill Centre, Faculty of Education Kenry House, Kingston Hill Kingston upon Thames, Surrey KT2 7LB 0181 549 1141	nlp/upm
Laban Centre for Movement and Dance Laurie Grove New Cross, London SE14 6NH 0181 692 4070	Dance
Middlesex University Faculty of Education and Performing Arts Bramley Road, Oakwood London N14 4XS 0181 368 1299	pr/sec
University of Greenwich (incorporating Avery Hill and Garnett Colleges) Bexley Road, London SE9 2PQ 0181 316 8444	nlp/upr/sec
The University of North London Prince of Wales Road, London NW5 3LB 0171 607 2789	pr/sec
University of the South Bank Caxton House 13–16 Borough Road London SE1 0AL 0171 928 8545	nlp/upr/sec
West London Institute of Higher Education Gordon House 300 St Margaret's Road, Twickenham Middlesex TW1 1PT 0181 891 0121	lpr/upr/sec

Name and address of institution	Type of course
Manchester Metropolitan University Didsbury School of Education Wilmslow Road, Manchester M20 8RR 0161 445 7841	nlp/lpr/pr/sec
Newcastle upon Tyne, University of Northumbria at Newcastle School of Education Studies Coach Lane Campus, Coach Lane Newcastle upon Tyne NE7 7XA 0191 232 6002	pr/sec
Newport, Gwent College of Higher Education College Crescent, Caerleon Newport, Gwent NP6 1XJ 01633 421292	nlp/upr/sec
Northampton, Nene College Moulton Park, Northampton NN2 7AL 01604 715000	nlp/upr
Nottingham Trent University Faculty of Education Clifton Hall, Clifton, Nottingham NG11 8NJ 0115 941 8418	pr/sec
Oxford Brookes University Headington, Oxford OX3 0BP 01865 819039	nlp/upr/sec
Westminster College (Meth)+ North Hinksey, Oxford OX2 9AT 01865 247644	lpr/upm
Sheffield Hallam University School of Education, 36 Collegiate Crescent Sheffield S10 2BP 0114 272 0911	lpr/upr/sec
Sunderland, University of Sunderland School of Education, Edinburgh Building Chester Road Sunderland, Tyne and Wear SR1 3SD 0191 515 2082	nlp/upr/sec

Name and address of institution	Type of course
Swansea Institute of Higher Education Townhill Road, Cockett, Swansea SA2 0UT 01792 203482	pr/sec
Wakefield, Bretton Hall College of Higher Education West Bretton, Wakefield West Yorkshire WF4 4LG 01924 830261	nlp/pr/m
Winchester, King Alfred's College (CE)+ Sparkford Road, Winchester SO22 4NR 01962 841515	lpr/upr/sec
Wolverhampton University Faculty of Education, Gorway, Walsall, West Midlands WS1 3BD 01902 321000	nlp/upr/sec
Worcester College of Higher Education Henwick Grove, Worcester WR2 6AJ 01905 748080	lpr/upm/sec
Wrexham, North East Wales Institute of Higher Education Cefn Road, Wrexham, Clwyd LL13 9NL 01978 290390	nlp/upr/sec
York, College of Ripon and St John Lord Mayor's Walk York YO3 7EX 01904 656771	

Northern Ireland

Queens University, University Road, Belfast BT7 1NN; 01232 245133

University of Ulster (Coleraine), Cromore Road, Coleraine, Co Londonderry BT52 1SA; 01265 441141

University of Ulster (Jordanstown), Shore Road, Newtownabbey, Co Antrim BT37 0QB; 01232 365131

University of Ulster (Magee College), Northland Road, Londonderry BT48 1ED; 01504 371371

Stranmillis College, Stranmillis Road, Belfast BT9 5DY; 01232 381271

St Mary's College, 191 Falls Road, Belfast BT12 6FE; 01232 327678

Name and address of institution	Type of course
Scotland	
Faculty of Education of the University of Paisley Ayr KA8 0SR 01292 260321	pr/sec
Faculty of Education at the University of Strathclyde Jordanhill Campus Southbrae Drive, Glasgow G13 1PP 0141 959 1232	pr/sec/FE
Moray House College of Education Cramond Campus, Cramond Road North Edinburgh EH4 6JD 0131 212 6001	pr/PE/BEd/Tech
Holyrood Campus, Holyrood Road Edinburgh EH8 8AQ 0131 556 8455	pr/sec
Northern College Aberdeen Campus, Hilton Place Aberdeen AB9 1FA 01224 42341	pr/sec
Dundee Campus, Gardyne Road Dundee DD5 1NY 01382 453433	pr
St Andrews College (RC) Bearsden, Glasgow G61 4QA 0141 943 1424	pr, sec
Stirling University Stirling FK9 4LA 017686 73171	BA, BSc plus Diploma in Education (sec)

University Degree Courses with an Education Content

The following universities offer first degree courses for BEd, or degrees in education combined with other subjects. You apply to these through UCAS, and they are listed in the *UCAS Handbook*.

Most of these are four-year courses including a graduate certificate. BA/BSc Hons three-year courses in education and other subjects, concerned with sport, library studies, English and drama are also available.

Bath: BSc Hons Education with a science subject.

Brunel: Bsc Hons with Industrial Design, Design and Technology, Natural Sciences.

Cambridge: BA Hons Education; Homerton College BEd.

Durham: BA Hons Education.

Exeter: BA(Ed), BSc(Ed) Hons Educational Studies.

Heriot Watt: BSc Hons Maths with Education.

Hull: Integrated Degree – BSc Hons Degree with Graduate Certificate in Education.

Keele: BA Hons with Certificate in Education.

Lancaster: BA Hons Educational Studies (with various options).

Liverpool: BSc Hons Mathematics with Education (four-year course with Graduate Certificate in Education).

London: King's College: BSC Hons Physics and Education with PGCE; Mathematics and Education with PGCE.

Loughborough: BA Hons. BSc Hons Industrial Design and Technology and Education; Information and Library Studies with Education, BSc Hons PE and Sports Science and another subject.

Manchester: BA Hons in Combined Studies. BSc Hons in Speech and Pathology.

Reading: BA(Ed) Hons Education and Community Studies.

Sheffield: BSc Hons Chemistry with Education.

Southampton: BSc Hons Mathematics with Education.

Stirling: BA Hons Education, BA Hons/Ord Education and another subject. BSc Gen/Hons Education and Science with PGCE. Home Economics, Sport and Leisure.

Ulster: BA Hons/BSc Hons Education or combined subjects.

Wales

    Aberystwyth: BA Joint Hons Education with another subject, BSc Joint Hons Education with Mathematics.

    Bangor: BA Joint Hons Education with another subject, BSc Joint Hons Education with another subject (Bangor Education courses taught in Welsh only).

    Cardiff: BA Hons Education with another subject.

Warwick: BA Hons Education and Philosophy, or Psychology, or Sociology; BA Hons with Teaching Certificate.

York: BA Hons Education and another subject, BA Hons Social Sciences and Education.

Postgraduate Certificate of Education (PGCE) Courses

English and Welsh institutions offering courses for the Postgraduate Certificate of Education. You apply to them through the Graduate Teacher Training Registry:

Aberystwyth, University College of Wales
Department of Education
Old College, Aberystwyth
Dyfed SY23 2AZ

Ambleside, Charlotte Mason College
University of Lancaster
Ambleside, Cumbria LA22 9BB

Bangor, Normal College
Bangor, Gwynedd LL57 2PX

University College of North Wales
School of Education
Bangor, Gwynedd LL57 1DG

Bath, College of Higher Education
Newton Park, Bath BA2 9BN

Bath University
School of Education
Claverton Down, Bath BA2 7AY

Bedford College of Higher Education
37 Lansdowne Road, Bedford MK40 2BZ

Birmingham University
Faculty of Education
PO Box 363, Birmingham B15 2TT

Newman College
Genners Lane, Bartley Green, Birmingham B32 3NT

Birmingham University of Central England in Birmingham
Department of Teacher Education and Training
Westbourne Road, Edgbaston, Birmingham B15 3TN

Bognor Regis/Chichester, West Sussex Institute of Higher Education
The Dome, Upper Bognor Road,
Bognor Regis PO21 1HR

Bradford and Ilkley Community College
Great Horton Road, Bradford BD7 1AY

Brentwood, Anglia Polytechnic University
Sawyers Hall Lane, Brentwood, Essex CM15 9BT

Brighton University
Faculty of Education Studies
Falmer, Brighton BN1 9PH
Eastbourne (PE)
Milnethorpe Court, Meads Road, Eastbourne, East Sussex BN20 7QD.

Bristol University
School of Education, PGCE Division
Helen Wodehouse Building, 35 Berkeley Square, Bristol BS8 1JA

Bristol University of the West of England at Bristol
Department of Education
Redland Hill, Bristol BS6 6UZ

Brunel University
Faculty of Education and Design
Runnymede Campus, Coopers Hill, Egham, Surrey TW20 0JZ

Cambridge, Homerton College
Cambridge CB2 2PH

Cambridge University
Department of Education
17 Trumpington Street, Cambridge CB2 1QA

Canterbury, Christ Church College
North Holmes Road, Canterbury CT1 1QU

Cardiff, College of Cardiff, University of Wales
Department of Education
Senghennydd Road, Cardiff CF2 4AG

Cardiff Institute of Higher Education
Cyncoed, Cardiff CF2 6XD

Carmarthen, Trinity College
Carmarthen, Dyfed SA31 3EP

Cheltenham and Gloucester College of Higher Education
(incorporating the College of St Paul and St Mary)
The Park, Cheltenham, Gloucestershire GL50 2RH

Chester College
Cheyney Road, Chester CH1 4BJ

Crewe and Alsager College, University of Manchester
Crewe, Cheshire CW1 1DU

Derby, University of Derby
Mickleover Campus, Derby DE3 5GX

Durham University
School of Education
Leazes Road, Durham DH1 1TA

Exeter University
School of Education
St Luke's, Heavitree Road, Exeter EX1 2LU

Exmouth, University of Plymouth
Rolle School of Education, Exmouth EX8 2AT

Huddersfield, University of Huddersfield
School of Education
Holly Bank Road, Lindley
Huddersfield HD3 3PP

Hull University
School of Education
173 Cottingham Road, Hull HU6 7RX

Keele University
Department of Education
Keele, Staffordshire ST5 5BG

Lancaster, St Martin's College
Bowerham, Lancaster LA1 3JD

Leeds Metropolitan University
Department of Education
Beckett Park, Leeds LS6 3QS

Leeds, Trinity and All Saints' Colleges
(Affiliated with the University of Leeds)
Brownberrie Lane, Horsforth, Leeds SL18 5HD

Leeds University
School of Education
Leeds LS2 9JT

Leicester University
School of Education
21 University Road, Leicester LE1 7RF

Lincoln Bishop Grosseteste College
Lincoln LN1 3DY

Liverpool Institute of Higher Education
Christ's and Notre Dame College
St Katharine's College
Stand Park Road, Liverpool L16 9JD

Liverpool, John Moores University
I M Marsh Campus
Barkhill Road, Liverpool L17 6BD

Liverpool University School of Education
PO Box 147, Liverpool L69 3BX

London
Kingston University
Kingston Hill Centre
Kenry House, Kingston Hill, Kingston upon Thames KT2 7LB

Middlesex University
Bramley Road, Oakwood, London N14 4XS

South Bank University
Dairy House, 77–81 Borough Road, London SE1 1DW

University of Greenwich
(incorporating Avery Hill and Garnett Colleges)
Faculty of Education and Community Studies
Avery Hill Campus
Bedley Road, Eltham, London SE9 2PQ

Roehampton Institute
Digby Stuart College, Roehampton Lane, London SW15 5PH

Froebel Institute College, Grove House, Roehampton Lane,
London SW15 5PJ

Southlands College, Wimbledon Parkside, London SW19 5NN

Whitelands College, West Hill, Putney, London SW15 3SN

London University
 Goldsmiths' College
 Lewisham Way, New Cross, London SE14 6NW
 Institute of Education
 Bedford Way, London WC1H 0AL
 King's College
 Centre for Educational Studies
 Cornwall House Annexe, Waterloo Road, London SE1 8TX

West London Institute of Higher Education
Gordon House, 300 St Margaret's Road, Twickenham
Middlesex TW1 1PT

University of East London
Longbridge Road, Dagenham, Essex RMB 2AS

University of North London
Department of Teaching Studies
Marlborough Buildings, 383 Holloway Road, London N7 0RN

Loughborough University of Technology
Department of Education
Loughborough, Leicestershire LE11 3TU

Manchester Metropolitan University
Didsbury School of Education
Wilmslow Road, Manchester M20 8RR

Manchester University
Department of Education
Manchester M13 9PL

Middlesex University
White Hart Lane, London N17 8HR

Newcastle upon Tyne University
School of Education
St Thomas Road, Newcastle upon Tyne NE1 7RU

Newcastle upon Tyne, University of Northumbria at Newcastle
Department of Education Studies
Coach Lane Campus, Newcastle upon Tyne NE7 7XA

Newport, Gwent College of Higher Education
College Crescent, Caerleon, Newport, Gwent NP6 1XJ

Northampton, Nene College
Moulton Park, Northampton NN2 7AL

Norwich, University of East Anglia
School of Education, Norwich NR4 7TJ

Nottingham Trent University
Department of Education Studies
Clifton Hall, Clifton, Nottingham NG11 8NG

Nottingham University
School of Education
University Park, Nottingham NG7 2RD

Ormskirk, Edge Hill College of Higher Education
Ormskirk, Lancashire L39 4QP

Oxford Brookes University
PGCE Course Admissions Registry,
Headington, Oxford OX3 0BP

Oxford University
Department of Educational Studies
15 Norham Gardens, Oxford OX2 6PY

Oxford, Westminster College
North Hinksey, Oxford OX2 9AT

Plymouth, College of St Mark and St John
Derriford Road, Plymouth PL6 8BH

Reading University
Faculty of Education and Community Studies
Bulmershe Court, Woodlands Avenue, Earley, Reading RG6 1HY

Scarborough, North Riding College
Filey Road, Scarborough, North Yorks YO11 3AZ

Sheffield Hallam University
36 Collegiate Crescent, Sheffield S10 2BP

Sheffield University
Division of Education
Arts Tower, Sheffield S10 2TN

Southampton, La Sainte Union
College of Higher Education
The Avenue, Southampton SO9 5HB

Southampton University
School of Education
Southampton SO9 5NH

Staffordshire University
College Road, Stoke on Trent ST4 2DF

Sunderland University
Edinburgh Building, Chester Road, Sunderland SR1 3SD

Sussex University
Education Area, PGCE Admissions, Sussex House
Falmer, Brighton BN1 9RH

Swansea, University College of Swansea
Department of Education,
Hendrefoilan, Swansea SA2 7NB

Twickenham, St Mary's College, University of Surrey
Strawberry Hill, Twickenham, Middlesex TW1 4SX

Wakefield, Bretton Hall College of Higher Education
West Bretton, Wakefield, West Yorkshire WF4 4LG

Wales, University of
(see entries for constituent colleges at Aberystwyth, Bangor and Cardiff)

Walsall, University of Wolverhampton
(West Midlands College of Higher Education)
Gorway, Walsall, West Midlands WS1 3BD

Warwick University
Faculty and Institute of Educational Studies
Coventry CL4 7AL

Watford, University of Hertfordshire
School of Humanities and Education
West Hall, Aldenham, Watford WD2 8AT

Winchester, King Alfred's College
Sparkford Road, Winchester SO22 4NR

Worcester College of Higher Education
Henwick Grove, Worcester WR2 6AJ

York, Ripon and St John College of Higher Education
Lord Mayor's Walk, York YO3 7EX

York University
Graduate Office
Heslington, York YO1 5DD

Music
If you have an approved qualification other than a degree, such as the graduate Diploma offered by the Royal College of Music, you can take a special PGCE style course to qualify you as a teacher. You should have five GCSEs (Grade C or above) or equivalent, including the standard English and maths qualifications.

These courses are available at:

Bath College of Higher Education
Birmingham University
Birmingham, University of Central England in Birmingham
Cambridge – Homerton College
Durham University
Exeter University
Leeds University
Liverpool Institute of Higher Education

London:
  Kingston University
  Middlesex University
  Roehampton Institute of Higher Education
  University of London
  Goldsmiths' College
  Institute of Education
Manchester Metropolitan University
Reading – Bulmershe College of Higher Education
Reading University
University College of Wales at Aberystwyth/Cardiff
Wakefield – Bretton Hall College of Higher Education

There are also courses at Dartington College of Arts, Totnes, and Colchester Institute of Higher Education.

The Open University

It is not surprising that the Open University has a high proportion of teachers among its students. Their background makes it relatively easy for them to follow a course of study on OU lines.

The Open University works through a programme of correspondence texts linked to radio and television broadcasts and Saturday Schools. Students have a local link with the University through regionally based part-time staff, and there are residential summer schools each year which usually form a compulsory part of the course. Students are also encouraged to form self-help groups to work together, especially where it is difficult to provide personal contacts with OU staff.

The University offers undergraduate, postgraduate and continuing education courses, many of which are not at degree level. The School of Education offers both undergraduate courses of interest to a wide audience and professional education courses for those already working in education. The OU is now offering a programme of part-time PGCE courses. These run from February to July the following year, and include 18 weeks of school experience. The programme offers primary courses for those wishing to teach ages 5–8 and 7–11 and secondary courses in at least seven secondary subjects.

The course aims to provide access to teaching through a part-time multi-media course developed through a partnership between the OU and schools. A big advantage for home study students is that they can nominate the school at which they would like to do most of their teaching practice, and the University will arrange this if it can reach agreement with the school. Students also get some experience in another school.

As well as the school experience and specified hours of personal study students attend Saturday day schools and five two-hour tutorials.

Applications

The OU publish a very helpful prospectus for their PGCE programme, obtainable from the PGCE Office, Open University, Walton Hall, Milton Keynes MK7 6AA; 01908 652996.

Qualifications for entry are the same as for any PGCE course, but the OU is particularly good at helping students to obtain the required qualifications. They also have a good record of supporting students with disabilities.

The same student grant and loan arrangements as for college teacher training courses apply. Tuition fees but not incidental expenses such as travel and materials, would normally be paid by the local education authority and there may be a small maintenance grant for those with low incomes.

Conclusion

The Open University presents a great opportunity for people who wish to improve their professional qualifications and, for one reason or another, need to study at home. But, as the OU tutors point out, 'It is not easy to study at home. You need a lot of will power – and the support of other people.'

Chapter 8
Further Reading

Higher Education

British Qualifications, Kogan Page, 26th edition, 1996 (£29.50)

Colleges and Institutes of Higher Education, Standing Conference of Principals and Directors of Colleges and Institutes of Higher Education, 1991. (Available free from Edge Hill College)

Compendium of Advanced Courses in Colleges of Further and Higher Education, Regional Advisory Councils (£4.40 post free)

Complete Degree Course Offers, Brian Heap, Trotman, 26th edition, April 1995, (£15.50)

DOG Guide to Postgraduate Study, Newpoint (£9.95)

Handbook of Degree and Advanced Courses, Linneys ESL, Newgate Lane, Mansfield NG18 2PA

The NATFHE Handbook of Initial Teacher Training, National Association of Teachers in Further and Higher Education (address as Linneys ESL above)

PUSH, (Polytechnic and University Student Handbook), Black Box Publishing (£9.99)

The Student Book, ed Klaus Boehm and Nick Wellings, published annually by Macmillan

UCAS Handbook – How to Apply for Admission to University, UCAS annual (free)

University and College Entrance: the Official Guide, UCAS, 1996 (£12)

Which Degree?, Hobsons, four volumes, annual

Teacher Training Agency (TTA)

The TTA is responsible for providing information and advice about routes into teaching and teacher training. It publishes a wide range of leaflets and reports, obtainable from the TTA Information Section, Portland House, Stag Place, London SW1E 5TT; enquiry lines for teacher training advice and literature 0171 925 5880; 0171 925 5882

TTA also publishes a regular termly bulletin, *Platform*, on the work of the TTA and also the work that schools and higher education institutions are doing in teacher education and to promote teaching as a profession

General

The Law of Education, Butterworth (reference only)

Education Yearbook, Longman Community Information, annual

'Talking about equal opportunities'; free from Publication and Marketing Unit, Equal Opportunities Commission, Overseas House, Quay Street, Manchester M3 3HN

Education Press

Education, journal for education administrators but of general interest to others in education. Weekly £1.75 on special order from newsagents or £74 per annum by post

The Times Educational Supplement, required reading for teachers. Weekly on Fridays from newsagents, price 90p

Term Time; jobs and general teaching interest newsletter for heads, governors and teachers in Greater London published by Timeplan, the supply teaching agency; 90p, twice termly
20–21 Arcadia Avenue, London N3 2JU; 0181 343 4043

Schools Update published by DFEE termly for all in education; circulated to schools and colleges, free from
DFEE Publications Centre, PO Box 6927, London E3 3NZ

National press

The Guardian has a particularly large education section on Tuesdays. Most other national papers have a weekly education page

Most of these papers will be available in your local reference library as will many of the expensive reference books. Many more specialist educational journals are listed in the *Education Yearbook*.

Chapter 9

Useful Addresses

Clearing House for Postgraduate Courses in Art and Design
Penn House, 9 Broad Street, Hereford HR4 9EP; 01432 266653

Department for Education and Employment
Sanctuary Buildings, Great Smith Street, London SW1P 3BT;
0171 925 5000

DFEE Publications Centre
PO Box 6927, London E3 3NZ; 0171 510 0150; 0171 510 0196 fax

Department of Education for Northern Ireland
Teachers Branch, Waterside House, 75 Duke Street, Londonderry BT47
1FP; 01504 319190 phone and fax

General Teaching Council for Scotland
5 Royal Terrace, Edinburgh EH7 5AF; 0131 556 0072

Graduate Teacher Training Registry
Fulton House, Jessop Avenue, Cheltenham, Glos GL50 3SH;
01242 225868

National Union of Students
461 Holloway Road, London N7 6LJ; 0171 272 8900

Open University
Walton Hall, Milton Keynes MK7 6AA; 01908 274066

RADAR
12 City Forum, 25 City Road, London EC1V 8AF; 0171 250 3222

Skill: National Bureau for Students with Disabilities
336 Brixton Road, London SW9 7AA; 0171 274 0565
Information Officer
0171 978 9890 1.30–4.30 Mon–Fri

TEACH: Teacher Education Admissions Clearing House
PO Box 165, Holyrood Road, Edinburgh EH8 8AT; 0131 558 6170

Teacher Training Agency (TTA)
Portland House, Stag Place, London SW1E 5TT; 0171 925 3700

UCAS Universities and Colleges Admissions Service
PO Box 28, Cheltenham, Glos GL50 3SA; 01242 222444

The Kogan Page Careers Series

This series consists of short guides (96–128 pages) to different careers for school and college leavers, graduates and anyone wanting to start anew. Each book serves as an introduction to a particular career and to jobs available within that field, including details of training qualifications and courses. The following 'Careers in' titles are available in paperback. Enquiries phone 0171 278 0433.

Accountancy (*5th edition*)
Architecture (*4th edition*)
Art and Design (*7th edition*)
Banking and Finance
  (*4th edition*)
Catering and Hotel Management
  (*4th edition*)
Environmental Conservation
  (*6th edition*)
Fashion (*3rd edition*)
Film and Video (*4th edition*)
Hairdressing and Beauty
  Therapy (*7th edition)*
Journalism (*7th edition*)
The Law (*7th edition*)
Marketing, Advertising and
  Public Relations (*5th edition*)
Medicine, Dentistry and
  Mental Health (*7th Edition*)

Nursing and Related Professions
  (*6th edition*)
Police Force (*4th edition*)
Publishing and Bookselling
  (*2nd edition*)
Retailing (*5th edition*)
Secretarial and Office Work
  (*7th edition*)
Social Work (*5th edition*)
Sport (*5th edition*)
Television and Radio (*6th edition*)
The Theatre (*5th edition*)
Travel Industry (*5th edition*)
Using Languages (*7th edition*)
Working Outdoors (*6th edition*)
Working with Animals
  (*7th edition*)
Working with Children and
  Young People (*6th edition*)

Also Available from Kogan Page

Great Answers to Tough Interview Questions: How to Get the Job You Want (3rd edition), Martin John Yate

How to Pass A levels and GNVQs (3rd edition), Howard Barlow

How to Pass Graduate Recruitment Tests, Mike Bryon

How to Pass Numeracy Tests, Harry Tolley and Ken Thomas

How to Pass Selection Tests, Mike Bryon and Sanjay Modha

How to Pass Technical Selection Tests, Mike Bryon and Sanjay Modha

How to Pass the Civil Service Qualifying Tests, Mike Bryon

How to Pass Verbal Reasoning Tests, Harry Tolley and Ken Thomas

How You Can Get That Job!: Application Forms and Letters Made Easy, Rebecca Corfield

How to Win as a Part-Time Student, Tom Bourner and Phil Race

Job Hunting Made Easy (3rd edition), John Bramham and David Cox

Making it in Sales: A Career Guide for Women, Mary J Foster with Timothy R V Foster

Manage Your Own Career, Ben Bell

Preparing Your Own CV, Rebecca Corfield

Readymade Job Search Letters, Lynn Williams

Test Your Own Aptitude, (2nd edition), Jim Barrett and Geoff Williams

Working Abroad: The Daily Telegraph Guide to Working and Living Overseas (18th edition), Godfrey Golzen

Working for Yourself: The Daily Telegraph Guide to Self-Employment (16th edition), Godfrey Golzen

Your First Job (2nd edition), Vivien Donald and Ray Grose